Lea
Skills that
Inspire
Incredible
Results

Leadership Skills that Inspire Incredible Results

FRED HALSTEAD

This edition first published in 2018 by Career Press, an imprint of
Red Wheel/Weiser, LLC
With offices at:
65 Parker Street, Suite 7
Newburyport, MA 01950
www.careerpress.com
www.redwheelweiser.com

ISBN: 978-1-63265-150-1
Library of Congress Cataloging-in-Publication Data
Names: Halstead, Fred, 1943- author.
Title: Leadership skills that inspire incredible results / Fred Halstead.
Description: Newburyport, MA : Career Press, an imprint of Red Wheel/
Weiser,
 2018. | Includes bibliographical references.
Identifiers: LCCN 2018022921 | ISBN 9781632651501 (pbk. : alk. paper)
Subjects: LCSH: Leadership. | Management.
Classification: LCC HD57.7 .H3454 2018 | DDC 658.4/092--dc23
LC record available at https://lccn.loc.gov/2018022921

Cover design by Kathryn Sky-Peck
Interior by Gina Schenck
Typeset in Minion Pro and Abadi Condensed Light

Printed in Canada
MAR
10 9 8 7 6 5 4 3 2 1

Acknowledgments

I'd like to offer special thanks to:

My wife, Donna, for her patience and support, especially over the past few years as this book was ever so slowly written. St. Augustine said: "Patience is the companion of wisdom," and she has both. Without her, this book would have remained a dream.

My children and grandchildren, Freddie, Julie, Scott, Amy, Ellie, Ashley, and Allie Cate, whose love and support is unconditional. I have listened to and learned from each of them.

Jeanne Glasser Levine, for her talent as an editor and her willingness to welcome my many changes in the manuscript over the past year.

Michael Pye of Career Press for his keen insights and intuition about how to use my thoughts and cause them to be even more appealing to you, the reader.

Judge Jay Patterson, a friend of fifty years and a talented writer, for his great encouragement and review of a very early manuscript.

Father Greg Methvin for his encouragement.

For my clients who have embraced the concepts and gave me the opportunity to hone them with practical applications. Key among this group are Jon Foster, Sylvia Young, Troy Villarreal, Heather Rohan, Gary Thomas, Mike Sanborn, Biggs Porter, Patti Niles, Kirk Metzner, and Mike Williams.

Kathy Light, who is a trusted, creative, and thoughtful partner in delivering the Skills That Inspire Incredible Results Program to leadership teams.

Contents

Author's Note

Beyond my experience and education, this book is an extension of a program called Skills That Inspire Incredible Results (STIIR) that I offer to leadership teams. As a result, the thoughts, concepts and suggestions have been tested by hundreds of executives. This book is meant to be a catalyst to help each reader become even more successful. It also can be used to help sustain, throughout the STIIR Program participant's career, the effective use of the six key skills.

Introduction

What could be the benefits for you as a person and as a leader if your words and actions come from a foundation of respecting others and a goal of making all those around you successful? Ralph Waldo Emerson said: "What we are speaks louder than what we say." Now modify that by one word: *Who* we are speaks louder than what we say. If you agree with that statement and want to be a person and a leader who thinks the right thing to do is to respect others and help others be successful, this book gives you straightforward, occasionally profound, and consistently practical ways to begin to achieve that, and in the process, achieve incredible results! Let's start with a story of a former client.

The client was a 44-year-old CEO of an organization with about 1,200 employees who had experienced great success during his first twenty years in business. Having been promoted many times, he initially thrived as a CEO, but after five years he found himself in a predicament: Despite having the same position in the same organization, his performance had declined. His boss was clearly not happy with most of the performance indicators, especially as the company faced a fierce new competitor. The CEO knew that to improve the numbers and prevail over threatening competition, it was necessary to develop a new company culture and do so with a heightened sense of discipline and urgency—there was no time to ease into change. In his mind, his job, and maybe even worse, his sense of self-worth—his ego—were threatened.

He knew that *everyone* is responsible for an organization's performance; teams don't succeed unless each person on the team succeeds, but that was not happening. Somehow, every individual throughout the organization needed to develop a greater sense of personal responsibility and accountability. Cultural transformation had to start with the CEO and the way he led and inspired others. To reach their performance goals, he would have to revolutionize his leadership style. It was a bitter pill to swallow. He had to change even though he thought his leadership and intelligence had led to the company's achievements throughout the past five years—and he thought it would do the same going forward.

Yet, after this tough realization and a growing sense of dread, he was willing and motivated to do whatever he needed in order to get the company back on track. He made the hard decision to change the core of his leadership style, not only because he felt he had to, but also because he knew he wanted to improve as a person and as a leader. The drive to improve became a personal quest. Just three months after his decision, everyone started to see the results: He started to transform himself, and as a result the executive team and the company were all transformed.

Improve the Fundamentals

So, what happened? The CEO sharpened some fundamentals that might on the surface seem deceptively easy to refine. But they are in fact difficult to alter because exceptional focus and discipline are required to change ingrained behaviors and habits. He challenged himself to greatly improve these abilities:

➤ Listen with purpose, focus, and curiosity.

➤ Encourage and inspire others through genuinely acknowledging them.

➤ Ask more on-target and powerful questions.

➤ Require others to develop their own solutions and action plans.

➤ Delegate with greater wisdom and thoughtfulness.

➤ Develop a culture of consistent accountability.

Polishing these skills so that using them fully and consistently became forefront in his mind required focus, discipline, and grit. But once they became habitual, his team began to emulate them. Within just six months, his subordinates started to set new expectations for their own direct reports. One additional thing he discovered was when he was intentional about respecting those with whom he worked, he was more clearly motivated to listen to them, to ask them what they thought, to delegate more effectively, and to hold them accountable rather than doing things himself or just giving them a pass.

Because of his new leadership approach, the CEO found he had more time to think. He was less stressed. His team leaders were finding their own solutions instead of relying on him, and they felt more responsible for the good results. Employee satisfaction and engagement increased. Internal quality indicators were at their highest recorded levels, as were company profits. This dramatic shift took place so quickly simply because the key leader made an important decision to rework the fundamental way in which he led.

As we discussed in the opening story, we see how the role of the leader impacts every aspect of company, team, and individual performance. The CEO's company was able to rebound because he improved the fundamentals and ensured that his employees did the same.

Inspire Change

Throughout the past thirty-eight years, first as an executive search consultant and then as an executive coach, I had the opportunity to learn in-depth about the leadership characteristics and styles of hundreds of executives. During those years, I became acquainted with only a few executives who demonstrated competence in the leadership approach discussed in this book. The approach includes skills that I strive to practice every day as an executive coach. And when leaders use them, they have a larger impact.

Leaders are unlikely to master *all* of these skills, but over time and with laser focus, they can use all of them to their—and others'—great benefit. Every one of my clients who have consistently followed the advice presented throughout these chapters inspired incredible performance changes in their direct reports. And in most cases the benefits carried over to their entire organization, and even to their relationships with their family and friends.

As a professional coach, my goal is to:

> ➤ Inspire senior leaders to grow and prosper as individuals and as leaders.

> ➤ Inspire teams of senior leaders to improve their performance levels as individuals and as cohesive teams.

This book will help you become a great listener and questioner, one who can inspire others, bring out their sharpest thinking, delegate with new purpose in mind, and consistently hold them accountable. *You will see how using every one of these actionable skills demonstrates your respect for others, and by shining the spotlight on others you will bask in the fulfillment of their accomplishments and your own incredible accomplishments.*

This book is meant to inspire you to improve these skills for yourself, then use them to inspire and help others around you. This book provides you with new insights and perspectives on what these skills are and how you can use them with confidence and create even greater success for you, for your team, and for the entire organization.

Throughout the book, as I provide practical and effective ways to improve as a leader, I use real examples from my work with senior executives, as well as experiences from leaders of top organizations and companies across a number of different industries.

One of the key goals of any leader is to energize and equip others to *achieve* exceptional results that exceed established goals. The leadership approach discussed throughout this book will help you accomplish exactly that. Executives who have actively embraced and used my leadership program, which is the backbone of the approach discussed here, have reported the following:

➤ Increased self-confidence among the leader's direct reports and their subordinates.

➤ Greater appreciation from direct reports and subordinates.

➤ More rapid development of subordinates' abilities.

7

➤ Higher levels of personal performance, with more people inspired to do their best work and thinking.

➤ Improved retention of the best talent.

➤ Consistent reports of subordinates completing assignments—on time.

➤ Increased ability of workers to use their experience and talents to the organization's benefit.

➤ A deeper sense of personal fulfillment.

➤ Improved performance metrics for the entire organization, including: net income, EBITDA, employee and customer satisfaction, greater market penetration, and quality.

➤ More energy and optimism about the future.

The advice in this book is sensible and, at the same time, exceptionally difficult to use consistently—the former isn't surprising, but the latter might be. Achieving perfection in the use of the skills I discuss is not a useful goal. Working to become much better at each one of the skills will offer incredible results. The journey, however, is not easy. Giving yourself some personal grace along the way will allow you to appreciate the incremental improvements and the results those improvements produce.

When reflecting on anyone's ability to truly master these skills, I am reminded of a T. S. Eliot quote: "For us, there is only the trying. The rest is not our business."

The Spotlight

For most of us, listening is not as natural and satisfying as talking; it helps to be honest about that. *Asking questions—in particular, questions that can inspire clearer thinking, solutions, and action plans—is challenging, especially when we are used to just telling others what we know should be done.* All of the executives I've coached are very capable people; most would attribute their success to their experience, intelligence, and ability to produce answers. This, understandably, offers some psychological fulfillment. I've heard many executives admit that it's rewarding to have the answers and to feel like the smartest person in the room. That's an honest and perfectly understandable feeling.

It is natural to enjoy expressing what you know or think you know. When a subordinate comes to you and asks for a solution to a problem, you may already have the best answer and solution in your mind, so you tell them. Being the authority and the smartest is a satisfying way to lead, but it creates missed opportunities for subordinates to grow in their thinking and in their career.

It also misses the opportunity to allow them to feel they are capable of arriving at the best solutions themselves. The opening story about the CEO illustrates just how impactful it is to the overall success of the company to have teams who are self-reliant, who understand the goals of the organization, and who can execute on those goals.

Asking the right questions is the most efficient and productive way to guide others to reach their own solutions and action plans. Yet, when telling rather than asking is ingrained in your everyday routine, switching gears requires real focus. It also requires you to understand what you will gain by changing your behavior and what motivates you to do so.

> "Always remember that asking the right questions brings out the best thinking in the other person, creating a sense of ownership that greatly increases the likelihood of success."
> —A client's observation

Although implementing a new leadership approach is a real challenge, it can create an incredibly positive change. One of the central goals of this book is to provide a new perspective on how the use of these critical leadership skills can create both personal fulfillment and measurable results in your performance and the organization's performance. As you read this book and practice these methods, you will see how you project your respect for your subordinates and the higher level of *self-confidence and overall performance* they will achieve.

During my years as an executive coach and as an executive search consultant, as I assessed and followed the careers of hundreds of senior leaders, I was able to observe the qualities of the most successful leaders. One of the qualities that seemed to stand out was a passion to change and to continue to grow as a person and a leader. Those who have that quality are the most secure and genuinely self-confident leaders. That quality is central to the message and purpose of this book.

Darwin said, "It is not the strongest of the species that survive, nor the most intelligent, but the one most responsive to change." As you evolve using the skills discussed in this book, you will cause people around you to perform at the highest possible level, and through your leadership they will gain even greater respect for and loyalty to you. Through your transformation, you will also find greater self-confidence and a sense of fulfillment than you thought possible. It begins with your openness to change. Think about the ways you can use the talents you were given to become more of the person and leader you want to be. Reflect on circumstances when your behavior is what you wish it to be, and what you can do or think to achieve the same attitude and behavior consistently.

> **Leaders who truly want others to succeed are the ones who achieve the greatest personal success.**

People are motivated to change when they understand that the gain is worth the challenge of adjusting their habits. Once people grasp the huge potential of a new way of thinking and acting, it becomes easier to face the potential roadblocks they may encounter along the way to any goal. As you read this book, pay particular attention to what benefits you will receive as a result of honing the skills discussed here. My clients discover that they become more like the person they genuinely want to be when they focus on using these skills.

Finally, although I worked with many leaders, it became apparent that *those who truly want others to excel are the ones who also achieve the greatest personal success.* As you use these skills, you will find yourself connecting with others as individuals in a new way. They will be more motivated to follow you because they realize you want them to thrive. By shining the spotlight on others, you will notice a positive change in all of your relationships, wherever they may be.

As you work to refine your leadership approach, please do not underestimate your capacity to use these skills effectively and, through their use, inspire others to achieve incredible results.

1

The Art and Joy of Listening

To be heard, first we must listen.

Years ago, I complied with my wife's request to have my hearing checked. She told me time and again that she felt I did not consistently hear her. I was surprised and somewhat reluctant, but decided to go to an ENT. Everything checked out and the doctor told me my hearing was fine. As you may have guessed, I realized it wasn't my hearing that was defective—it was my listening. That event accelerated my interest in making listening a hallmark for me, not only as a coach, but in all aspects of my life.

The Proactive Listener

That experience may explain, in part, why I named this chapter "The Art and Joy of Listening." Yes, you can gain joy and satisfaction from demonstrating respect for others by really listening to them. In this chapter, we will explore the benefits of truly listening, then explore listening inhibitors, and finally, what you can do to become a better, proactive, and an effective listener. We inherently know that we benefit *from* listening to others, but most of us have never thought about what will motivate us to become great listeners. What benefits do we truly receive and how do they help us both professionally and in our personal lives?

There are five main advantages to becoming a great listener. Some of them are direct, while others are by-products:

1. Learn.

2. Show respect and express appreciation for others.

3. Stay out of trouble.

4. Achieve the best thinking and the best results.

5. Be a fully connected listener.

Let's take a moment to walk through each one so you better understand their importance. Keep in mind that you may not experience all of these benefits at once, rather they will develop over time as you hone your ear—and your behavior—to truly listen to others. You will, however, quickly find some positive, immediate results when you stop talking, pay attention, and listen closely.

Learn

Most leaders have an inquisitive mind, and being inquisitive is one of the foundations for effective listening. When you listen to others, you gain a deeper appreciation of their ability to think critically, develop ideas, and provide solutions to problems. You both support others' best thinking and quench your thirst for knowledge and understanding. As you hear someone walk through their thought process and fully explain their positions or actions, you gain an appreciation of what people around you have to offer. In the process, other questions or thoughts may arise, which contributes to your becoming more inquisitive.

> **When listening, we become more aware of what**
> *we can learn from just about anyone.*

The opportunity to learn is most obvious when we listen to someone we respect and consider wise and knowledgeable. But when I open my mind, I also find that I learn from my children, grandchildren, people I casually meet, and even people who initially do not appear to be particularly smart or wise. When listening, we become more aware of what we can learn from just about anyone. Many people surprise me with what they know if I truly listen to them. If you stay inquisitive, keep an open mind, and shut out personal barriers, you will be amazed by how much you can learn by actively listening.

Show Respect and Express Appreciation for Others

We all want to be respected and appreciated, and we naturally appreciate those people who respect us. When someone expresses appreciation for the person you are as well as the position you hold, a bond and mutual admiration is created. To create such a positive environment, it is imperative that you listen to your team, and that they listen to you. This sets the stage to inspire and motivate each other. Although being appreciated and respected is more important to some people than others, all of those to whom you show your appreciation and respect by listening will be far more inclined to follow you as the leader and reciprocate with their respect for you.

How many times have you sensed a person whom you greatly respected was listening to you—focused on you alone? When this happens, your confidence typically grows as you feel respected and your work valued. Conversation opens up and your motivation to continue to express yourself as thoughtfully and clearly as you can increase. What are your thoughts about the people who listen to you and engage in meaningful discussions? I find that mutual respect is created, and I am more willing to candidly speak about any type of issue or problem I'm facing. I respect and admire everyone who I coach. As I ask clients questions and listen to them, they sense my respect and become comfortable in expressing thoughts that they may be reluctant to share with others. They know that I listen without judgment. As you truly listen to another person with full engagement, your personal confidence grows and you become more confident in the other person's abilities as well. When you show respect by listening carefully to others, they are likely to do so with their fellow leaders, employees, clients, and others with whom they come in contact.

> **"The opposite of talking isn't listening.**
> **The opposite of talking is waiting."**
> **—Fran Lebowitz**

How do we respond to a person who actively listens to us and is interested in what we know and what we think? We appreciate and value that person. How often have you said or thought something such as: "He (or she) is a person that listens to me"? We feel valued and respected and therefore value that person who truly listens. *Why is it easier to follow and respect a person who listens to us? One of the most important reasons is that we in turn feel respected and valued.* What are the implications if you become known as a person who listens to everyone with respect and genuine interest?

Many leaders whom I have coached cannot think of one person who has genuinely and consistently listened to them. This creates a breakdown in communication, ill will, and negative attitudes and outcomes. If you are willing, however, to be the person who listens, who shows respect through giving someone your undivided attention, you will be revered. People will respect you more and trust your opinions, motivations, and actions.

An article by Elizabeth Bernstein published in the *Wall Street Journal* titled "How 'Active Listening' Makes

Both Participants in a Conversation Feel Better" supports this notion. In the article, Ms. Bernstein refers to research done by Dr. Graham D. Bodie, associate professor of Communication Studies at Louisiana State University, who found that "...when the listener displayed more of the (immediacy) behaviors [such as] making eye contact, paraphrasing, asking open-ended questions—the talker perceived the listener as more emotionally aware, and felt better. The verbal behaviors, on average, were three times as likely as nonverbal behaviors to produce this outcome."[1]

Stay Out of Trouble

In all aspects of your life, how many times have you been in trouble or not met expectations because you did not listen? Examples with your spouse can easily come to mind. Most people don't want to even think about tallying that number!

How many times have you thought, "If I'd just listened, I wouldn't have this problem"? This happens in professional settings every single day. Misunderstood project requirements, failed contract negotiations, or lack of clarity around performance goals spring to mind.

Problems created by not listening are avoidable. Yet, it's so easy to tune people out—some in particular! Our personal filters thwart our listening. A significant aspect of hearing sounds, in contrast to really listening, comes from clearing away our personal filters so that we hear what another person *actually* said, rather than what we *think* they said.

Achieve the Best Thinking and the Best Results

Achieving the best thinking and results is a key aspect of this book. The most effective and powerful questions lead to actionable achievements and positive outcomes. They provide insight into a project or dilemma, and help people collaborate more productively. *To ask powerful questions, and gain the desired results, listening must come first.* It's natural to think you need to prepare your questions in advance of an important interaction or meeting. This method is especially valuable as you come up with questions in the context of what you want to accomplish and also helps inspire others to achieve what *they* need to accomplish.

However, a significant problem in focusing solely on your questions is the increased likelihood of not really listening because you are thinking about what you want to say or ask next. For most people, it seems strange and improbable not to think about the questions you plan to ask as you listen to another person. But as you listen to others and absorb what they are saying and thinking, questions will come to mind. *As you become a more attuned listener, you will notice that you do not have to spend as much time thinking in advance about what questions you will ask; they will just come naturally as a result of your focused, unfiltered listening.* The desire to have an immediate response or fix the person's problems quickly, as well as the need for "efficient communication," leads you away from focused listening. There is no need to interrupt the speaker with your thoughts on what is being said—until the time is right. Verbal cues even as simple as "I see," "Mmmhmm," or "Go on," will foster an environment that encourages the speaker to keep talking. That is what unfiltered listening looks like. And, yet people will go down rabbit holes and use far too many words to express a thought, we will later discuss ways to keep others on track and discussions productive.

While you are listening, questions based on what you heard, your sense of curiosity, or what is missing from what the other person is saying will come to mind. As you consider what someone is telling you and how you can guide and help that person to expand their thinking and their knowledge, the powerful questions will flow naturally. (I'll cover this topic in the chapter on asking powerful questions.) When you listen first, then ask questions, you create a dialogue that leads to results.

Action Step

As you go into a meeting with your team, your goal may be to simply give them the cut-and-dry information they need to perform a task or duty. Yet when you ask some key questions and listen to them first, you'll find that they too have a great deal of information and knowledge that will affect your judgment and plans.

Think about what else you can accomplish. One important thing may be to engage them immediately to gain their thinking and buy in. Although this may seem like it would take too much time, once you start doing it, you will find it to be highly efficient.

More than Hearing

If you just think of hearing what the other person has to say without considering how you can help them achieve the best results through careful listening and questioning, and how they can help you and the overall team with this goal, you miss the chance to lead them in a highly significant and effective way. If you just hear the words without hearing what the person actually intends to say, you will miss the opportunity to gain the essential clarity and results you seek. And when you start listening objectively, instead of listening to hear what might be wrong with what they are saying, you'll see a big difference in your and their success.

Listening to others establishes your role as an effective and empathetic leader, one who keeps an open mind and is willing to learn from others, no matter their level in the organization or their perceived worth or value. This environment results in mutual respect and appreciation, while steering you clear of misunderstandings or negative feelings and helping your team and overall business reach new heights. So, if the benefits are so clear, why doesn't every leader take this proactive listening approach?

> "The most important thing in communication
> is hearing what isn't said."
> —Peter Drucker

Be a Fully Connected Listener

Listening is a contact sport. It is not for the weak. Great listening requires a real connection between you and the other person or people. Great listeners hear what is in the other person's mind and heart. Through listening and questioning, they make a real, almost tangible connection. You might be surprised when your goal is to make a lasting connection with another person just by really listening to them.

Listening Inhibitors

There are many inhibitors to listening and understanding what another person is actually saying. Several of these barriers reflect our attitude toward others, but they also shine a light onto our own personal feelings, biases, and shortcomings. In any professional setting, our ego tends to play an outsized role, especially if we are in a leadership position. As a leader, you may find that your preconceived notions or unwillingness to learn from others ends up inhibiting your performance overall. When you fail to listen, you fail to understand. This lack of perception will create barriers in your personal life, career, team effectiveness, and business goals. To avoid these issues, first understand the specific listening inhibitors you're up against, and then learn how you can overcome them. I have found the primary inhibitors to be:

> The natural desire to talk.

> Judging others.

> Preconceptions and biases.

> Ego.

> Multitasking.

> Shutting people off.

"There is a kind of listening with half an ear that presumes I already know what the other person has to say. It is an impatient, inattentive listening that despises the brother and is only waiting for a chance to speak and thus get rid of the other person."
—Dietrich Bonhoeffer, *Life Together*

The Natural Desire to Talk

We want to create a favorable image. We want to appear knowledgeable, smart, and aware. Those things feed our ego and self-esteem. When we think about what our response will be to what we hear, our ability to focus on what is really being said is diminished, as is our ability to pick up on any nuance or meaning the talker wants to convey. It might seem impossible to carefully listen and at the same time appear to the other person as smart and knowledgeable. It might also be difficult to imagine that you can focus on and listen to the person and, just through listening, develop insightful questions.

Put your curiosity into overdrive! Those insightful questions will demonstrate your engagement and intelligence. If you find yourself thinking about what questions to ask when you are "listening" to another person, start thinking about what will motivate you to focus only on what you are hearing. Your motivation may be that you will miss learning something useful or you will project a lack of respect for the other person, or a list of other possibilities. Armed with a better understanding of your personal reasons for becoming a proactive listener, you will have the ability to more easily listen and, as a result, ask great questions.

One of the ideas that is often discussed in my individual coaching exchanges is the process of thinking about all the ramifications of what one wants to gain from any interaction or meeting. When you open up your mind to doing more than giving directions, so much more is possible. Your goals in a meeting can include inspiring, encouraging, and motivating your team and helping them understand the level of importance or priority of the topics discussed. You can also work to gain trust in each other. None of these goals are possible to attain, however, unless you listen first and then ask questions.

Judging Others

Everyone judges the actions and words of others, and doing so is an essential part of leadership. I refer to that sort of judgment as "assessing"—assessing one's thoughts and actions. Assessing is a critical part of leading people and helping them achieve the desired results. "Judgment" as in judging another person's value, beliefs, intelligence, personality, or background, however, inhibits listening. We are all guilty of this type of judgment at one time or another. I have yet to meet a person who, if honest, will not admit to judging other people's nature rather than assessing only what they say or do. The fact is, most everyone tends to judge people on surface assumptions and there is no easy cure for such snap conclusions. As with anything we wish to change, self-awareness and honesty is a good place to start.

> "In order to sense the deeper meaning and purpose people are seeking, leaders have to listen. They have to listen not just with their ears, but also with their eyes and hearts. Leaders hold up a mirror and reflect back to their followers what they most desire."
> —James Kouzes and Barry Posner, *Christian Reflections on the Leadership Challenge*

When a person says something we think is incorrect, naïve, or flat-out wrong, we tend to hastily conclude that the person's input or contribution is worthless. We react negatively and are even dismissive of the speaker. In doing so, that individual feels personally judged, a feeling that can act as a curtain being drawn between the speaker and the listener. The listener then loses the benefit of the knowledge the speaker had to offer and mutual respect and appreciation between the two break down. There are millions of not-so-bright ideas or thoughts, but very few people *who have absolutely nothing to offer*. Regardless, everyone deserves the same amount of respect that we, too, would hope to receive.

When you feel as if you are *not* being judged, it's likely you can express your thoughts clearly and achieve your best thinking. You can also concentrate on your best thinking rather than on whether the listener values you personally or not. The same idea applies to any other speaker—they will be more open and more productive if they feel that you are listening to what they have to say. As a leader, the dividends are great when you discipline yourself to think and express more positive responses in your words and facial expressions. If you disagree with someone, you want to give the impression that you believe his thought or plan is an "ill-advised idea," not that you consider him a "dumb person." And for many people, it is easy to conclude that when another person attempts to communicate that it was a wrong-headed idea, that the person indeed thinks you're communicating he or she is stupid. So be clear with your words if you wish to try to gain the person's best thinking. For example, you might ask: "What would make that an even better idea?" or "What do you see as the possible pitfalls with that idea or plan?"

Although judging others is a common practice, with resolve we can slowly and incrementally resist judging others' character and value. Motivation for change might come from any number of sources. As one who works hard to follow the teachings of Christ, I am motivated by the Christian belief that it is God's place and not mine to judge others. Even so, it's a struggle. A significant part of my job, and yours, is absorbing information and ideas and then assessing them. *The real challenge is to actively assess thoughts and ideas without judging anyone's person-ality and beliefs, or as a particular type or class of person.* This challenge, more than most, requires discipline and focus. As you listen to another person, ask yourself: "Is my judgment of this person blocking my ability to hear and assess what they think?" If it is, then ask: "What are the consequences for that person and for me?"

When coaching an executive, one of my initial steps is to conduct an in-person 360-degree assessment during which feedback is solicited from the executive's peers and colleagues. This is an effective way of allowing the client to see his or her image as others see it. It helps the person become more aware of his or her strengths, as well as tar-get areas in which change could be particularly helpful. One of my observations during a 360-degree assessment of a client, who had responsibility for several billion dol-lars in revenue, was that a number of people believed he was judging their character and other personal attributes during their conversations and meetings. They were fine with him assessing their ideas, but when he seemed to be judging them personally, their respect and trust for him diminished.

Most of us have had similar experiences. If you have been fortunate to have a boss who did not judge you personally and who trusted you as a person, you likely felt motivated to strive to perform at your highest level. Lack of personal judgment demonstrates trust. *When a follower feels trusted, his or her best thinking and performance are given the wings to soar.* As indicated by the findings in a follow-up 360-degree assessment of the same client, I found that his peers and colleagues felt that his overly judgmental attitude and practices had improved. Part of his ability to make that difficult change came through reflecting on the few people he did not judge and understanding what helped him to resist passing such swift judgment.

He then figured out ways he could use his new insights as he thought about those he was judging. Also, as he thought about his core beliefs and who he wanted to be as a person, judging others did not fit his values. This insight reinforced his motivation to make the difficult change. Although it might seem impossible to avoid judging others, doing so yields a great impact on your ability to listen, and in turn on your leadership behavior.

When we skillfully and thoughtfully assess others' thoughts and actions, rather than judging them, we inspire them to change and grow. Try this: The next time you find yourself "sizing up" or judging someone, notice how that inhibits you from grasping what they are saying and thinking and from inspiring them to achieve a much higher level of performance.

Judging others can place us on a slippery slope. When we carefully assess others' thoughts and actions, rather than judging them based on their personalities or perceived value, we inspire them to change and grow. When we judge others' character or worth as a person, intentionally or not, our ability to listen to and understand their thoughts is substantially diminished, and we stifle their best thinking and energy, creating a hurtle for them to achieve their best work and contribute to the success of the overall team.

Preconceptions and Biases

A source of our judgment of others comes from our preconceptions and biases. When my clients talk about their struggles to truly listen to certain people, they often have some preconceived notions about that person. Some of these notions can be harsh, relying on deep-seated prejudices and ingrained thought patterns that may not truly be connected to reality. It's common for us to rely on base assumptions, even against our best intentions. How often have you thought, "He's not very smart," "She doesn't know much about this," or "How can anyone who looks like that be intelligent?"

Leaders also have a tendency to think that they've "seen it all" or "heard it all" before. If you're in senior-level management, in addition to your knowledge and aptitude, your experiences have obviously played a major role in the ascension of your career. You may therefore find yourself quickly dismissing someone based on your prior experiences with a similar person. For example, if you have worked with a colleague who was new to operations and found that the learning curve was too difficult, you may think that anyone new to such a position won't be able to perform the necessary duties appropriately. In response, you feel that they have no credibility with you. Or say you have had negative experiences with a member of a sales team in which they seemed to not understand your core product or services. You may end up writing off the rest of the sales team, thinking that they too have little knowledge of what they're actually selling.

Preconceptions are akin to self-fulfilling prophecies. With preconceptions, we see through a preprogrammed filter—not what is there, but what we expect to be there. "I know this person *always* has this bias." "I know she *never* prepares adequately." "He's part of a functional area of a company (or a state or region of the country) and they all think alike." As you ignore your preconceptions about a person, a person's position, or a group of people, and truly listen and ask questions to bring out their thinking, you may learn that they are smarter and more capable than you thought and that your previous experiences don't always apply to the current realities.

Unless we discard the filters we have created, we will always see a person in the same way. We think they never change, even though they do. We think they never grow as leaders, even though they do. By truly shattering those preconceived notions, a leader can take full advantage of what that person offers and give him or her the respect and confidence to thrive. We all develop preconceived ideas about other people. The trick is to first be aware of those preconceptions and then realize what affect they have on our ability to really listen to, understand, and assess what is being said without a bias.

Do you know someone who causes you to struggle to see and hear past your preconceived notions? Do you already think you *know* what that person will say rather than taking the time to listen to what he or she really is saying? What would be the benefits for you and for that person if you disciplined yourself to squash those preconceived notions and truly listen to that person? As we

In the past forty years of listening to, interviewing, assessing, and coaching hundreds of executives, I have concluded those who have a big ego are more insecure than those who are humble. My experience is that those who are most secure in who they are, those who have a deep and genuine self-confidence, are the ones who most easily listen to, respect, and value others.

Judging others, relying on preconceptions—or misconceptions—and personal bias, and fluffing up our ego, no matter how slightly, are all related, and they all keep us from being the best listeners, and in turn thinkers, that we can be. But there are other considerations that inhibit our listening that are not tied to our ingrained personality traits.

Multitask

Our ability to think comes from our prefrontal cortex lobe. Information we learn is processed serially, meaning that each piece of new information is processed individually. Our brains cannot take in multiple pieces of information simultaneously. Some people do, however, have the capacity to process information rapidly, but it is still one bit at a time. Most people in today's overworked, hyper-speed society feel that it is imperative to do as many things as possible at once: check email while driving,

rely on our preconceived notions and biases, we inhibit our listening, and our performance suffers. No matter how hard we try, those preconceptions may linger, but ignoring them and focusing on the potential positive outcomes that are elicited by proactive listening will help us move forward. Still, it can be tough due to aspects of our personality that feel like they're out of our control, such as our ego.

Ego

It is hard to admit that ego plays an outsized role in many of our motivations, decisions, and actions. Our ego can prevent us from really listening to people whom we think are intellectually or socially inferior to us. Conscious or subconscious thoughts of *I'm superior* or *I'm smarter* get in the way of respecting, appreciating, and listening to others. Our egos lead us to believe that we are smart—maybe the smartest person in the room. That is an essential notion and will be key in our continuing success, especially when you have a good understanding of how you are smart and when you attribute your intelligence to God-given gifts. But when leaders let their egos reign supreme and assume they are smarter than everyone else, they will be more prone to making overarching judgments and uninformed decisions that will reduce their effectiveness. And worse, it can diminish the capabilities of those around us, those very people on whom our success is predicated. This might seem intuitive, yet all of us have at one time thought, "What can I possibly learn from this person about this subject or any subject?" As my clients have discovered, fighting through this inhibitor will yield dividends.

"Smart" people have no need to prove how smart they are. People around them will notice their intelligence. When we—consciously or unconsciously—send a signal that says, *I'm smarter than you,* we shut down the other person's desire to produce his or her best thinking. If a follower thinks his leader is proud of her superior intelligence, he's likely to concede, without challenge, to that leader. The stifled, silent follower remains reticent, and both parties lose. The follower then becomes either increasingly dependent on his leader or increasingly resentful of her.

One example of this situation can be seen in Virginia, an accomplished executive for the past twenty years. She enjoys interacting with her peer executives and subordinates. Most people liked her and would say she is engaging and able to relate well to others, but has a strong

need to be viewed as intelligent. She didn't underst the impact of her ego until she underwent a 360-de assessment. As a result of the assessment, she lea that the more she talked, the less value each of her w had. Her peer executives thought she was not intere in their feedback because of her strong belief that she right (even when she wasn't). She suffered from a la respect—the thing she most wanted.

> **The less we worry about appearing smart, the smarter we**
> **appear to be by just listening and asking smart questio**

Over time, her understanding of the results behavior, coupled with a greater understanding talents and how she could use them more fully and tively, helped her change and become more of a k of the company's executive leadership team. She l that the more she put aside her ego and truly listen less she talked. And the more questions she ask more she would be respected and appreciated by one with whom she worked. In the process, she more self-confident and less ego-driven. As she more self-confident, she became a better listener. creased self-confidence allowed her to listen n talk less.

respond to a text in the middle of a meeting, juggle ten projects at once, or read emails during a conference call that are unrelated to the content of the discussion, making them unable to give any task the attention it truly deserves or needs. The hustle and bustle of the contemporary work world leads us to believe multitasking is the end all and be all, which has major implications on how we listen to one another.

> "You cannot truly listen to anyone and do anything else at the same time."
> —M. Scott Peck, *The Road Less Traveled*

How often do you hear someone say, "I'm good at multitasking and proud of that ability"? Do you regularly think if you didn't multitask, you wouldn't be able to survive? Think of one person who, when you are talking, pays close attention to you and what you are saying. You can tell that they are solely focused on you and willing to give you the time and support you need. It is likely that you have a good working relationship with him and that you share mutual respect for one another. This person sends the message that you are important and valued—that your time is important. But what about the listener who seems absent, aloof, or thinking about something else when you're in the middle of a conversation? What message do you get when the "listener" is actually *doing* something else while you are talking, such as taking a call when you're in the middle of a sentence? How does she make you feel and how well do you work with her on a regular basis?

When we attempt to listen while multitasking, we can fool ourselves as well as discourage and disrespect the other person in the conversation. We convince ourselves that we have fully heard the other person, even when we haven't. In some cases, we may have listened to most of what was said, but we limit the opportunity to further explore the fullness of the person's thoughts and ideas. We make it clear that we have other things to do that are as or more important than listening to them. In the process, we disrespect the other person, as we are clearly showing them that they are not important enough to have our undivided attention.

When you're concentrating on solving an issue or facing a dilemma and someone interrupts you, consider saying this to the interrupter: "I want to focus on you, and I need to finish this right now, so let's postpone the discussion until I can fully concentrate on you *and* what you are saying." Two positive things happen that outweigh postponing the discussion. First, the person feels respected and honored that you're giving him or her your full attention. Second, you know that the person may become motivated to be better and more fully prepared next time to articulate his or her thoughts. You are signaling that they are important and that their opinions matter to you. Since that's the case, you are willing to give them your time and attention, even if it isn't right at that moment.

A participant in a program I offer that teaches stronger listening said:

> It is amazing. When I stopped multitasking when someone was talking to me, I really started listening and I could tell the difference. My kids and my husband were more expressive and I more naturally asked questions about what they were saying. The same is true of my subordinates and peers. And, in fact, I learned that one of my subordinates was smarter than I thought. I am shocked that I am actually saving time by not multitasking and just listening.

Can you experience the same results? Try this: For at least one month, any time someone is talking to you, focus your eyes, ears, and mind on that person, no exceptions. Turn away from any electronic device or anything else that has your attention so that you see only the person who is talking to you. Observe the person's reaction and assess your thoughts about that interaction. Alleviate the issues surrounding multitasking and figure out a way to measure your increase in focused listening.

Shutting People Off

When we disagree with what someone is saying, it's easy to quickly conclude that we will not learn anything useful from that person. Therefore, we only superficially listen, while thinking about how wrong the person is, how right we are, and how we can adroitly express our superior thinking (the ego inhibitor). So, we miss the fullness of the other person's thoughts and diminish our ability to learn from him or her. We concentrate on our *disagreement* rather than on the kernel of truth or the insight the other person might offer. We mentally reject the person's thoughts, and, in a sense, the person as well.

> **"Be quick to hear and slow to speak."**
> **—James 1:19**

One of my clients had this challenge. He failed to listen to the person with whom he was disagreeing, and then became frustrated. The result was: *Rather than listening and asking questions, he just told the person what to think and what to do.* It is important to note that such a dismissal can result in a cascade of missed opportunities to listen, hear, learn, inspire, motivate, and create a higher level of performance. (We'll explore how to put a stop to this behavior in the next chapter.)

We've all been there. Many times, it's not just that we disagree, but because we're sure we know what the other person will say, we see no point in listening. What if you are right and the person is predictable, but then he goes on to say something new while you have shut him off? You may lose out on critical information or knowledge that can help your entire team improve. In Chapter 3, the discussion will be about asking powerful questions. Developing a curiosity about and respect for others—and asking powerful questions—can lead to surprising answers from those you presume to be predictable.

But before you begin asking powerful questions, you must first be willing to put aside your disagreements and assumptions. When you rely on assumptions, you are more likely to interrupt or talk over the person who is trying to explain something to you. People *love* to hear their own voices and we all fall in the trap of speaking more than listening. In doing so, we shoot people down and shut them out, creating a cyclical effect. The more you talk, the less you listen. The less you listen, the less people will want to speak with you. The less people want to speak with you, the more you lose.

Another client of mine, Harry, is a bright and engaging person. People like him. Yet, he tended to talk and talk, rarely pausing so that others might express their thoughts. He didn't acknowledge that the cause of this shortcoming was his lack of confidence. But, indeed, to talk less and pause at appropriate times, he needed to gain more confidence in his ability to respond to differing thoughts and ideas. He was shutting people out—inhibiting conversations and his own proactive listening—without realizing it.

Although Harry made other changes that benefited his peers and subordinates, the one that benefitted them and him the most was talking less and listening more.

Throughout the course of six months, Harry started to gain more self-confidence as a result of understanding and using more fully his natural talents and developing them into strengths. The other factor that helped him was gaining a better understanding of his verbosity and the downside of talking without pauses (like his peers tuning him out and missing the important things he say-ing). Armed with those insights, he started the difficult effort of reminding himself to pause so that others might speak. He also sought to be more succinct, to ask ques-tions, and then to *listen*. As a result, his peers' and sub-ordinates' respect for him increased; he was recognized for being more thoughtful; and the performance of the operations he led improved substantially. To top it off, he was promoted a year later.

Harry's journey from incessant talker to patient lis-tener wasn't an easy one. In fact, it isn't easy for anyone. Whether it's your arrogance, assumptions, lack of gen-uine self-confidence, or unwillingness to stop talking, you create a negative environment that is not conducive to open, honest, and important discourse. And, maybe most important on a personal level, you will not be re-spected by others as you could and should be.

When you do achieve the ability to listen proactively, you then have a much higher probability of becoming a leader who can inspire others. Another way to inspire others is by asking them powerful questions—questions made powerful, in large part, because you first listened. You hear not only their words, but what their heart and mind were communicating.

2

Become a Great Listener

The sheer act of listening speaks volumes that even a great speech can't communicate.
—John C. Maxwell

Talking is natural for us. Listening is not. Talking is fun and can seem fulfilling and, yet, listening is essential and can be even more rewarding than talking. We will explore some of the things that will help you become a great listener and some of the rewards of listening we might not have thought much about.

Listening is, of course, a function of the brain. We need ears to hear the words so that the brain can give those words meaning. So, to be an effective listener, our brains must be engaged. Just hearing the words is not enough. We need to process what the speaker is saying while also considering the circumstances at the time they are spoken. Hearing is the fuel and the brain is *the engine that drives us to a place of understanding.*

I had a political science professor who was a master at engaging his students; as a result, we all enjoyed his classes. He encouraged his students to think and clearly express their thoughts. When he thought a student's logic was faulty, the professor would say, "I hear you," and move on to the next student. I always took that to mean, "I hear the words, but my brain suggests they are not worth processing." How many times have you heard the words and decided that they were not worth processing? This is another challenge in becoming a consistently great listener.

Becoming a great listener requires dedication and hard work. Some people may *think* that they are naturally born with such a talent, but it is only truly developed throughout many years of practice. It takes desire and motivation. (There will be more on motivating factors later in the book.) At the most basic level, we are required to listen with the clear intention of attempting to understand what the other person is saying. Each word someone says carries importance and gravity, explicitly or implicitly. And behind each word, there is a meaning that you must comprehend. When we notice the tone of the speaker's voice, their body language, and the lens through which we interpret these factors, we start to gain the ability to really listen.

It's complex, but once you get over the inhibitors and embrace the benefits of listening, you will learn more, share mutual respect between you and your colleagues, and reach new heights of success that you may have thought impossible previously. You will be grateful for the impact your improved listening has on you and others. It all starts with the benefits of an inquisitive mind—your curiosity is essential to the art of listening. Being curious is one of the key elements to actually *being* a great listener. In addition to curiosity, other habits you develop in order to make focused listening a part of your behavior are:

➤ Knowing and believing in your purpose for listening.

➤ Truly focusing only on what the other person is saying.

➤ Heeding the words, the inflections, the body language, and what is *not* said.

➤ Signaling that you are listening.

➤ Avoiding listening in debate mode.

➤ Learning how to ask great questions.

Be Curious

Albert Einstein said, "I have no special talents. I am only passionately curious."[1] Einstein looked at the world in a way no previous scientist ever had. His knowledge was vast, but to his own admission, it was only a byproduct of his curiosity. It's easy to lose sight of the power of curiosity. We all have varying degrees of curiosity and express our curiosity in different ways. Most of us need to push ourselves to stay curious. When we do, we will find our work more fulfilling, our conversations more enriching, and our ability to listen and learn heightened.

You most likely have heard that the most successful people in science, education, and virtually every kind of business have an active sense of curiosity. They want to learn about the world around them, understand new and exciting ideas, and use their ever-growing knowledge to excel. *Healthy curiosity is a key trait of the best listeners and is an important ingredient in developing effective listening.* This trait, more than all others, directly relates to the development of an inquisitive mind. If you stay excited about learning, doors of all kinds will open up to you—in the organization where you work and in your own success as a leader. The joy of truly listening is that we know we are learning, we know we are truly respecting the other person by listening, and by intensely listening we are inspiring them to continue to communicate clearly and thoughtfully.

> **"Curiosity is the wick in the candle of learning."**
> **—William Arthur Ward**

Like listening, expressing curiosity is also a way of signaling that we care about and respect another person. Curiosity fosters sharper thinking and inspires us to delve deeper into the subject at hand. When you express your curiosity about something a person says, does, or thinks, you signal that you care about what that person *says, does, or thinks*. That expression of caring inspires one's best performance and loyalty to you. Not only will you personally be affected, you will also affect your team and colleagues through your demonstrations of respect for them.

A unique perspective on the benefit of curiosity is the *curiosity quotient* (CQ). The primary hallmark of CQ is having a hungry mind. Even though CQ has not been as fully explored and tested as other measurements, such as IQ and EQ, Tomas Chamorro-Premuzic writes in the *Harvard Business Review* that

> [P]eople with higher CQ are more inquisitive and open to new experiences. . . . They tend to generate many original ideas and are counterconformist . . . [and] there's some evidence to suggest it is just as important when it comes to managing complexity in two major ways. First, individuals with higher CQ are generally more tolerant of ambiguity. This nuanced, sophisticated, subtle thinking style defines the very essence of complexity. Second, CQ leads to higher levels of intellectual investment and knowledge acquisition over time . . ." This love of knowledge is the very essence of active listening where you're hungry to learn what the other is thinking and has to say.[2]

John Maxwell says leaders lose their curiosity due to insecurity, low self-esteem, arrogance, contentment, and distractedness. That is a strong statement. There is the temptation, as you become comfortable in your leadership role, to feel that it is no longer necessary to expand your knowledge. Subconsciously it is tempting to think

"I've *made it*, so why do I need to listen to anyone else?" Without giving it a great deal of thought, it is apparent that a key component of success derives from listening to and learning from others. Possibly less apparent is how much more successful we would be in all aspects of our lives if our desire and ability to listen grew tremendously, or perhaps even just a little bit. As you demonstrate your respect for and interest in another person by expressing your curiosity and willingness to listen, your inquisitive mind's appetite is whetted, and your ability to listen grows. Of course, staying curious and sharpening your inquisitive mind is only the first step to becoming a great listener.

> **Listening and curiosity are the fertile soil in which great questions and learning grow.**

Know and Believe in Your Purpose for Listening

Although maintaining a mindset of curiosity and a joy in learning is an excellent starting point, it is critical to know that your purpose for listening can create actionable or tangible results. So many opportunities can arise if you listen with a purpose and a goal in mind. And when you know and understand your purpose for listening, you are far more likely to be motivated to do the hard work of truly listening. Intense listening is not easy!

An extension of knowing your purpose for listening (often discussed in my individual coaching exchanges) is thinking about all of the ramifications of what one wants to gain from any interaction or meeting.

The number-one thing that people typically seek in a meeting is information, yet there are many other purposes. For example, when you listen to someone, you learn how that person thinks, which provides insight into how you can use them most effectively on a project, team, or in the organization. If one of the purposes is continued assessment of a team member's talents, you want to intentionally listen with your specific assessment in mind. You may find that one of your team members is much more analytical or creative, or good at finding common ground or figuring out the pitfalls in a plan than you had originally thought.

When you are intentional about what your motives are for listening to another person, you will become a better listener and everyone will gain so much more from your effective listening.

Action Step

Try this: For the next month, keep a journal that details your purpose, motivation, and goals for actively listening in each meeting. After each meeting, see if you have reached your goals. Goals can be general, such as showing your respect to the whole group or showing your respect for each person by truly listening to them. You may also want to think of one person from whom you would like to hear more and allow that person to articulate his or her best thinking and solution. Make notes about your successes and missed opportunities to truly listen. As the journal grows, and you begin listening with your clear purposes in mind, you will see your success as a leader grow.

Thinking deeply about what you want to accomplish and your purpose for each meeting, whether it is with your team, an individual, or a large group will inspire everyone with whom you meet. Before your next meeting, create your goals for that meeting and think about what effect it would have on your ability to be a great leader and to inspire others.

Focus Only on What the Other Person Is Saying

Our minds appear to be programmed to wander. Our brain gives us distracting thoughts every seven to ten seconds! We think about what we will say or ask so that we will appear smart. We also think about what we will be doing in an hour, or a week, or next month, or on our vacation, or what we'll be eating for our next meal. There are so many things to clutter our minds. To focus solely on what a person is saying can be a tremendous challenge. The best listeners and leaders, however, have trained their brains to ignore distracting thoughts and concentrate on what is truly being said.

We have all noticed that we're able to focus with greater ease with specific people and in specific environments and not nearly as well in other environments. As an example, I can focus on what my clients are saying, whether listening to an individual client or a team of executives. With other individuals and groups, I need to focus on my purpose for listening and use that to motivate me to concentrate more deeply to make sure I understand what is being said. Having observed many clients and having listened to their stories, it has become clear to me that purposeful listening creates the difference between going through the motions of listening and gaining the most from what each person is saying and, even more importantly, through what you have heard them say, ask them questions that will inspire their best thinking.

Earlier, I discussed motivations to help you become a better listener, whether to help others to succeed or show genuine respect. When you embrace the purpose behind your listening, focus becomes easier. You will also take advantage of each moment you spend with someone, realizing that living in that moment rather than the future leads to more focused listening.

Heed the Words, Inflections, Body Language, and What Is Not Said

What others say or what they intend to say or want to say are often quite different. What is then actually heard or understood is different still. After you've improved your ability to truly focus solely on what is being said, it is then necessary to consider what you do *not* hear during a conversation—those words that are nuanced or unsaid.

Professor Emeritus of Psychology at UCLA's Clark University, Albert Mehrabian is considered to be a pioneer in the area of nonverbal communication. Dr. Mehrabian's background in engineering and natural science encouraged his approach to psychology. It is this background that led to his pioneering work in the area of nonverbal communication. Mehrabian famously provided metrics to the way people react to verbal (what is said), vocal (inflection), and visual (body language) communication. His work underlies the importance of what is said, vocal inflection, and body language. He found that:

> ➤ 7 percent of the message relating to feelings and attitudes are in the words that are spoken.

> ➤ 38 percent of the message relating to feelings and attitudes are in the way the words are said, which is in the inflection.

> ➤ 55 percent of the message related to feelings and attitudes are in facial expression and body language.

Observing body language is a key part of becoming a great listener, as is picking up on the fluctuations in someone's voice. When I coach over the phone, of course I can't see body language. But in phone consultations I have noticed that voice inflections are powerful indicators of what my clients want to communicate. The voice and body language are extensions—and actually amplify— the meaning of the words.

Once some knowledge of and rapport with another person is established, I believe phone exchanges can be as productive as in-person meetings. When you are a focused listener over the phone, you are more fully attuned to the words used, to inflection and tone. In fact, the acuity of your listening may increase because you do not have visual clues. You also are not distracted if the person you're speaking with makes any unusual facial or body movement (though these are important in their own right during face-to-face meetings). When you listen intently, you can hear concern or joy in the speaker's voice without seeing it on his face; you sense the emotion. Think of this type of listening as "listening with the Ray Charles affect." Because he could not see, all of his other senses were always elevated.

As strange as this might sound, the next time you are distracted from listening by the speaker's appearance, mannerisms, and so on, imagine you are blind and all you can do is listen to the words, the tone, the inflections, and the emotion in the person's voice. How much better would you be at listening? Or the next time you are on a conference call and distracted by your computer or the buzz around you, imagine you are Louis Brandeis, the former US Supreme Court Justice (who was blind) and are listening to lawyers give their oral arguments on a critical case. You cannot see anything; you can only focus on what it is that you are hearing.

Help Others Listen to You— The Power of the Pause

Just as reading body language and taking note of voice inflections will help you become a great listener, another powerful tool to understand and implement when necessary is the *pause*. In my coaching, I ask questions the client has not considered before, ones that require fresh thinking. A long period of silence often follows the question as the client processes his or her thoughts. Allowing long periods of silence can feel uncomfortable for most people. So, discipline to resist filling in the silence with another question or giving the answer is required. Although silence may feel awkward, the responder appreciates the time to think without interruption. It is a rare experience when a person wants to hear what we think badly enough that they will give us time to express our thoughts without prompting or leading us. *Honoring periods of silence while a person thinks sends a clear message that you respect that person.*

The best listeners never appear to be in a hurry. As the writer Fran Lebowitz said, "The opposite of talking isn't listening. The opposite of talking is waiting."

When I help executive teams hone these skills by demonstrating them during an exchange with the CEO in the presence of the team, the feedback on the silence is noteworthy. We discuss a challenge the CEO is currently facing, with the goal to create greater understanding of the challenge and formulate a solution. It is typical to have some periods of silence as the CEO forms his or her best thinking in response to the probing and challenging questions asked. At the end of the exchange, I ask the executive team what they observed. Inevitably, one of the observations relates to the periods of silence when the CEO is processing his or her thoughts.

The team members wonder if the periods of silence were awkward for the CEO. When the CEO is asked for his or her thoughts about the silence, the typical first response is something like this: "I felt some pressure to respond." The second response is typically, "I appreciated the time to form my thoughts."

> When we're great listeners, we give others the gift of silence. We're not in a hurry, so silence—time to think—gives the speaker the opportunity to formulate and express her best thinking.

Being Heard—The Power of the Pause, Part 2

Think about what it takes to be heard—to make it easier for your followers to actively listen to you. There are a number of factors that make listening easier. Some of those factors are being succinct, using stories to illustrate your point, speaking with conviction in your voice, and saying things that are of significance to your listener in a way that captivates their interest. One additional factor, when communicating to another individual or a smaller group, is pausing occasionally as you speak. We all know people who talk without pausing. Whereas some may have interesting, even vital things to say, we struggle to maintain active listening mostly because we are engaged in listening and we want to ask a question or make a clarifying comment. We want it to be a genuine two-way discussion. When we talk without even pausing for a second, we risk losing or maybe even turning off our listener. Be cautious about delivering uninterruptable monologues that last more than a minute or two in one-on-one or small team/group communications.

Send Listening Signals

During a 360-degree assessment interview for a client, one of his subordinate executives said, "I cannot tell if he is listening to me. He just stares at me without any expression. It can be maddening and unnerving." In a simplistic way this is analogous to the old question: If a tree falls in the forest and no one hears it, did it really make any sound? My client, upon hearing the feedback, said, "That is strange because I do listen. I am just concentrating on what others are saying." The point is: If you want to inspire others by intensely listening to them, you must send signals that you are in fact listening. They can be as simple as a smile, a nod, or a question based upon what you just heard. On the negative side, responding with the word "but" and then giving your thoughts signals clearly that you were not listening or did not value what the other person said. Try to use the word "and" instead of "but." In your mind as well as theirs, think additive rather than contrary. When a person says "but" after we have said something it can signal to us that they disagree and therefore we need to defend what we said. We are now more focused on being on guard and defending ourselves than we are on listening. After listening to someone, think about what it says about you when the first word you use is "but."

Feedback on Whether You Did or Didn't Listen

If you listened, heard, and understood what another person said, how will that person know? What are the consequences of the speaker not knowing if he or she was heard and understood? We have all experienced people who seem to be listening, but then give us cues that suggest they were preoccupied. If showing respect for the person to whom you are listening is one of your objectives, it is worthwhile to signal to that person you in fact did hear and understand. What are some of the best ways to do that? One is to repeat the thought they expressed (but not necessarily the exact words) back to them. This can be very effective, but it also has its limitations, as it can easily be overused, seeming almost robotic. Here are thirteen additional behaviors that will help you to become a better, more focused, listener[3]:

1. Restate: To show you are listening, repeat what the person said by paraphrasing what you heard in your own words. For example, "Let's see if I'm clear about this . . ."

2. Summarize: Bring together the facts and pieces of the problem to check understanding. For example, "So it sounds to me as if . . ." or, "Is that it?"

3. Minimal encouragers: Use brief, positive prompts to keep the conversation going and show you are listening. For example, "Umm-hmmm," "Oh?," "I understand," "Then?," "And?"

4. Reflect: Instead of just repeating, reflect the speaker's words in terms of feelings. For example, "This seems really important to you . . ."

5. Give feedback: Let the person know what your initial thoughts are on the situation. Share pertinent information, observations, insights, and experiences. Then listen carefully to confirm.

6. Emotion labeling: Putting feelings into words will often help a person to see things more objectively. To help the person begin, use "door

openers." For example, "I'm sensing that you're feeling frustrated, worried, anxious . . ."

7. Probe: Ask questions to draw the person out and get deeper and more meaningful information. For example, "What do you think would happen if you . . . ?"

8. Validation: Acknowledge the individual's problems, issues, and feelings. Listen openly and with empathy, and respond in an interested way. For example, "I appreciate your willingness to talk about such a difficult issue."

9. Effective pause: Deliberately pause at key points for emphasis. This will tell the person you are saying something that is very important to them.

10. Silence: Allow for comfortable silences to slow down the exchange. Give a person time to think as well as talk. Silence can also be very helpful in diffusing an unproductive interaction.

11. "I" messages: By using "I" in your statements, you focus on the problem, not the person. An "I" message lets the person know what you feel and why. For example, "I know you have a lot to say, but I need to . . ."

12. Redirect: If someone is showing signs of being overly aggressive, agitated, or angry, this is the time to shift the discussion to another topic.

13. Consequences: Part of the feedback may involve talking about the possible consequences of inaction. Take your cues from what the person is saying. For example, what would be Sylvia's reaction to expressing it in that way? Or what should be the consequences of not completing the project on time?

Listen in Debate Mode

Listening is also most effective when we are concentrating on what the speaker is saying, instead of mentally preparing for a debate or to prove the other person wrong. If your only purpose is to show that you are right and the other person is wrong, or to prove that you are smarter than him or her, it is impossible for you to listen. You will be unable to hear or value what the speaker says. That is often the outcome when we want to win the debate and walk away, pleased about how smart we are. It is like the old expression "Do you want to be right, or do you want to be married?" The new expression could be "Do you want to demonstrate you are smarter than the other guy, or do you want to be an inspiring and motivating leader?" When a person's mind is in debate mode, he or she is listening for and focused on flaws, not on what can be learned. When you listen with the goal of expanding the best thinking on the subject, it is easier to hear what the person is actually saying.

As discussed, becoming a great listener isn't easy— it takes determination and effort, curiosity, purposeful listening, focus, and awareness of what is left unsaid. As you work on these things, becoming known as a good listener will be easier. You will find a sense of joy in the art of listening because your sense of connection with your colleagues, friends, and family will deepen. When you listen carefully, you fully grasp what is said, and you can respond thoughtfully and productively. You ask better questions and a meaningful conversation ensues.

The Connection Between Great Listening and Great Questions

People who ask questions that seem to get to the heart of an issue are almost certainly good listeners. Whether the person is a great conversationalist, or a leader who asks incredibly astute questions, much of their ability to do so comes from listening and responding to what they understand from what they have heard. Questions signal that you heard what the person said. Think of what the positive effects would be of using a question to repeat the thoughts the other person suggested. In this process, you may suggest some cautions to be aware of in implementing the speaker's suggestion. In doing so, the speaker's idea is explored in more depth—and you are still talking about his idea rather than getting distracted by another topic. You listened and he or she knows it, and you encouraged the other person to expand his or her thinking.

Yet, many people struggle to ask the right questions and facilitate effective conversations. In the next chapter, we'll explore how and when to ask powerful questions and how to use them to generate results for you and your team.

3

Ask Powerful Questions

The wise man doesn't give the right answers,
he poses the right questions.
—Claude Levi-Strauss

David is a person whom I admire. He has a wonderful ability to engage people when he first meets them and to carry on a conversation with anyone. The talent lies not so much in his ability to win others over by the force and charm of his personality, but in something else. I asked him years ago to what he attributed this ability. He said it is simply a result of listening and asking questions. In other words, as you listen and ask questions, you become engaging. As that happens, people will more naturally want to listen to you and respect you.

On the other end of the spectrum, a client named Herbert found himself in an expanded role in which it was even more necessary to interact in a relaxed setting with customers he did not know well or at all. He was uncomfortable and did not feel in control when he needed to engage them in what he termed "small talk." By convincing himself that he was not good at small talk, he actively fulfilled his own self-evaluation. We explored what he needed to do to be at ease when relating to others through conversation. We first discussed the talents and characteristics he already had to help him become more engaging. With his direct reports, he had shown a sense of curiosity and the ability to ask them questions that brought out their best thinking on a variety of issues and challenges.

As he realized he had clearly already demonstrated the ability to use those talents, he gradually became more comfortable and at ease in making small talk (i.e., engaging) with his customers. Initially, it was a struggle. His questions were not directly business related, which was out of his comfort zone—he thought they felt a bit contrived. Yet, as he disciplined himself to ask questions—to listen and be curious—he found he was getting better at engaging his customers on a more personal level, which positively impacted his business relationship with them.

> **Asking questions engages people in conversation and creates bonds because you are showing your interest in them.**

Another client, Audrey, was concerned that one of her key direct reports was not capable of high-level performance in his job because he rarely took initiative or expressed what he thought. After asking her more about the relationship with this subordinate and the key aspects of his job, I asked her to tell me about a typical discussion with him. Audrey related that she had done most of the talking during their exchanges and had never, it seems, asked her subordinate any questions other than "Do you have any questions?" And he would respond, "No, boss," which was the answer he thought she wanted. I asked, "What would be gained from focusing on asking him questions to bring out his thinking before you tell him what *you* thought?" Audrey was not sure, but she agreed to try it. She struggled and felt awkward asking questions since she was so accustomed to being the dominant party in a business meeting, yet as she asked more questions, she slowly began to see that he did think clearly, he did have some good ideas, and he might be more capable than she previously thought. Because of Audrey's willingness to change her approach, over a period of a few months he went from a D player to a B+ player in her mind.

These examples show how questions can have a significant impact in different settings. Asking questions engages people in conversation and creates bonds because of your showing your interest in them and respect for them. When we ask a person questions and listen to that individual rather than just telling him or her what we think, we may learn that that person is smarter than we thought, has great value to add, and can contribute more to the team than we may have previously considered. Questions lead to insight and productivity—they help get things done! With the right motivation and focus, you can learn to ask powerful questions. Every leader has the capability to become known for their ability to use questions to achieve great and sometimes even implausible results.

> **Powerful questions asked at the right time and in the right way will create incredible results.**

John Maxwell said, "Never solve a problem for a person, solve it with that person."[1] *The best way to solve a problem with a follower is to ask them questions that direct them and draw out their best and sharpest thinking.* Though you likely ask hundreds of questions a day, the questions discussed here are those meant to elicit powerful responses and create a productive dialogue. Powerful questions have unique characteristics and purposes, and when asked at the right time and in the right way can produce results that are nothing short of incredible. Whether during an important meeting or presentation, when on-boarding new employees, or in the process of solving a major problem, they will help you generate your best thoughts and solutions. Let's start by discussing exactly what I mean by "powerful questions."

The Characteristics of Powerful Questions

Peter Drucker may have put it best when he said, "The most serious mistakes are not being made as a result of wrong answers. The true dangerous thing is asking the wrong question."[2] So what are the characteristics of powerful questions? A powerful question is one that will be on target with the subject being discussed and will move the ball forward to meet the objectives; it is the "right" question to ask. *The right question is often a crystallizer. It helps to put a bow of clarity around one's thoughts.* It will often help the person you're speaking with clarify their thinking and better articulate what they already know. It also can expand their thought process or cause them to discuss a complexity they have not considered previously.

> A powerful question has the ability in a positive and constructive
> way to steer and expand the other person's thinking.

Powerful questions are directly related to what you hear during a conversation and the relevant facts. They epitomize one's focus in that moment and target the bull's eye of relevance to the real issue at hand, especially if the real issue has not yet been addressed—which very often it has not. A powerful question has the ability in a positive and constructive way to steer or direct the other person's thinking. For example, sometimes the person with whom you are speaking is lost in the complexity of an issue because there are so many variables or moving parts that he or she cannot see what the solution is. In such a situation, you can help them lift that fog and create a clearer vision with a question such as, "What is at the heart of this issue?" Other "defogging" questions include:

➤ What concerns you most about this?

➤ At this point, what *does* seem clear about the challenge at hand?

➤ If there is one thing you could do to begin to resolve this issue, what is it?

➤ As a starting point, what needs to be done?

➤ What are your instincts telling you?

➤ What is the most important thing you want to come from this?

These questions can refocus the person to the fundamentals of the problem they're facing. Through your powerful questions, you allow the person to continue to own the challenge while helping them develop clarity about the solution. Why? As Jack Welch pointed out in his book *Winning*, "Before you are a leader, success is all about growing yourself. When you become a leader, success is all about growing others."[3] The right questions that zero in, explore, and penetrate the heart of an issue also provide a highly effective way to demonstrate your understanding of the matter, oftentimes better than directly expressing your thoughts. Many times, others have attributed greater knowledge and insight than I thought I had because of the questions I asked. You will have the same result. Asking probing questions is a key aspect of critical thinking. The Foundation for Critical Thinking underscores this importance: "Questions define the agenda of our thinking. They determine what information we seek. They lead us in one direction rather than another. They are, therefore, a crucial part of our thinking."[4]

Another key element of a great question is that it is formed and comes as a result of listening. When we first listen and *then* ask, and listen some more and then ask more questions, clearer and better thinking emerges. One without the other leaves some of the best possible thinking left undiscovered.

Of course, coming up with the right question isn't always so easy. These questions are only useful if they are asked at the correct time and in the appropriate manner. If they are not, then they will lose their power or totally miss the intended target or desired outcome. So, it's not just the "right" question, but how and when it is asked that leads to creating the best thinking and the best solutions, and it keeps people executing the plan on the course to achieve the needed results.

Ask a Question at the Right Time

Timing is an important characteristic of powerful questions. Knowing the right time to ask the right question requires acute listening and mental engagement. You must be able to read the particular person with whom you're speaking to know when it is the best time to continue listening or pause to ask the questions. Keep in mind that these questions will require the other person to clarify her thinking or to redirect or rechannel her flow of thoughts, so you need to make sure she is asked at the right time to give her the ability to think through the question you have asked.

For example, during my coaching exchanges I may feel like I am interrupting the client to clarify or slightly redirect. When asked later if they felt like I was interrupting them, the answer has always been no because they believe my question was a natural extension of what they were expressing. I was listening to them and they knew it. Questions asked at the right time may feel like you are interrupting the other person and that may well be the case. But it also might be the exact right time to ask the question to stay on point and to expand their thinking. When the person we are listening to seems to get off course, it is in their best interest to rechannel them. Although there are valid times for a person to have a cathartic stream of consciousness, those times are infrequent in everyday business conversations and should naturally be minimized.

Powerful questions that sometimes interrupt a stream of thought will help the person steer their thinking toward productive, action-oriented thoughts and language, or a new way to think about the issue being discussed.

They will be related to what that person can control; what he or she can do personally to directly solve the issue. The questions will often be positive in nature, such as, "What do you see as the benefits of what you are advocating?" This question causes the person to think out loud about the value of his plan and possible shortcomings in his thinking.

Timing depends upon several variables: the flow of one's thoughts, the intensity of the communication, the developing thought patterns, and your experiences with the receptivity of the other person.

> **Powerful questions hit the bull's eye of**
> **creating clarity and understanding.**

As mentioned, there is a right time to interrupt the flow of thoughts by asking questions that put the person back on target or steer them toward a solution—it also helps them see what they personally can do to solve the challenge. One of the best times to ask a question is when greater clarity is needed. *Powerful questions hit the bull's eye of creating clarity and understanding.* That bull's eye is a moving target, so the right time to launch the question can be critical. Intense listening, including vocal cues, is essential in knowing the right time to ask a question. For example, can you detect doubt in his or her voice? Is it possible to hear an overabundance of conviction? Does sounding doubtful send the message that you need to ask even more positive questions? Or is that how the speaker's analytical process works? Is being overly convicted the speaker's normal behavior or does it signal an underlying anxiety?

Understanding the baseline behaviors while listening intently will help you learn to discern when to interrupt the flow of a developing thought or to wait until the person has fully expressed him- or herself. If your goal is to bring out the best thinking of the other person, in contrast to telling them what you know or think, the right time to ask a question will be part of a natural flow of thoughts.

Earlier in the book, I made the point that when we are great listeners, we are not in a hurry. Silence while the other person is thinking is good for them and for our understanding of their best thinking. It is an interesting fact that when we slow down, we often can save time. It is natural to want to get to the answer, the solution, and the action plan as fast as we can. Yet, when we take the time to continue to ask pertinent, on-target questions, a better solution and plan will emerge. The best thinking and plan developed by thoughtful questions will reduce the need for costly changes and save time in bird-dogging the execution of that plan. You cause the person to own the thinking, own the plan of action, and have a natural accountability for the results.

However it's not just the timing that is important. Try to make sure you're asking the question in a way that will resonate with the other person and lead to better results. Before we go on to discuss the most effective way to ask questions, I would like to take a moment to note something to the readers who have the tendency to talk extensively and without pausing: You may well be missing the opportunity to engage the listener—an opportunity for them to actually hear you. And, in fact, you may have lost your listener who might be thinking things like:

➤ "Where is she going with this?"

➤ "That does not seem right."

➤ "He won't take a breath so I can ask a question."

➤ "I may be finished listening long before she is done talking."

Interestingly, for some people, it may also signal that you do not want to be contradicted or for anyone else to say anything on the subject. It can mean that you are unsure of yourself so you just keep talking. It also can indicate a lack of personal discipline and respect for the listener(s). When the long and fast talker finally asks, "What do you think?" the listener may be thinking, "I am not sure—with all that smoke, what is on fire is tough to discern."

What Is the Right Way to Ask a Question?

As an executive search consultant and coach, I have asked hundreds of leaders thousands of questions. Three of my goals were always to stimulate an honest and thoughtful answer, to challenge their thinking, and to learn from their answers. To accomplish these three goals and others, there are four types of questions I avoid:

1. Questions that can be answered with a yes or a no.

2. Questions that start with "why."

3. Multiple choice questions.

4. Questions that lead the person to what I think is the "right" answer in a way that limits their thinking.

Questions that elicit a yes or no answer can provide you with useful information. They do not, however, require any expanded thinking or the ability to learn more about the subject. They also may limit a person to respond only to *your* thoughts, instead of delving into or expressing their own. As an example, you might ask: "Is this the solution?" That has the possibility of limiting the best thinking about the issue. More powerful questions are: "If there were an even better solution, what would it be?" or "If there was one thing that would make this solution better, what is it?" The first question opens the door for them to think about it more, but then closes the conversation off. The second and third questions nudge them through the door and require them to consider what really is the best solution and it shines the light on them.

> **If you offer it, it is yours.**
> **If they offer it, it's theirs to own.**

Questions that start with "why" have a tendency to put people on the defensive—they ask people to defend their thinking rather than explain it in a positive way. "Why" questions tend to flatten out thinking. They cause the person to focus inward rather than devise a solution to an issue or spark ideas—something that would come out of a "what" question. Asking a question like: "Why did you do that?" has the risk of asking the person to defend his or her thinking or actions. Asking questions like: "What were your thoughts to reach the decision or take that action?" or "What might have been an even better way to do that?" ask the person to explain and expand his or her thinking and actions. The *why* question can have the effect of shaming the person. The *what* question has the effect of inspiring the person to express his or her very best thinking. Getting to and articulating the "why" of your business will have a tremendous impact on the ability to inspire others. Simon Sinek effectively makes that case in his book *Start with Why*. My experience suggests that the most effective and sure way to get to the "why" is to ask questions that begin with "what" because they encourage freedom of thought. So, to get the most clarity around the "why," ask questions that start with "what."

Another type of question that does not require expansive or best thinking is the multiple-choice question. When you provide potential solutions for the person you're speaking with, you limit the possibilities of finding the actual best solution. For example, say you ask someone in your office (let's call her Sue) about her thoughts on a major new initiative your company is rolling out. You tell Sue that you are really interested in her thoughts on the topic (such as, what are the most important things the company should do as a new initiative is started), but then follow that statement up with the question "Should we do A, B, C, or D?" Sue may have plenty of thoughts on what the company should do as the new initiative is started, but she is limited in her response due to the way you have posed the question.

When we ask a multiple-choice question, it can make us feel good to indicate to the person we're asking the question of that we have thought about the answer and that we are good thinkers. Let people know how smart you are by asking smart open-ended questions, not by giving them what you think the answer might be. That is an understandable goal. It also might be even wiser to ask yourself: "What are the advantages of eliminating multiple-choice questions from your lexicon?" The most evident one is: If you really want to gain the other person's best thinking, you give them the gift of thinking openly without any bias from you. When you ask multiple-choice questions you also may be perceived as thinking the other person is not smart enough to think of all the possibilities you did. When you ask an open-ended question and the person misses a key point or option, it's easy and quick to ask: "What are your thoughts about the point or option that you have thought about?"

Similar to yes/no questions, avoiding multiple-choice questions conveys respect and an honest desire to understand the position of the person you're having a conversation with. Ask them what they think without any filters. You may be pleased by what you learn about the subject and the person.

Powerful questions will almost always start with What, What, What! They are open-ended and non-restrictive, so they encourage the person to fully express his or her best thinking. "What" questions will generally contain no emotion, which evokes a sense that one needs to defend him- or herself as questions that start with "why" can. Questions that begin with "what" are simply non-accusatory. For example:

➤ What is your best thinking about . . . ?

➤ What is the best solution?

➤ What are the benefits of what you are proposing?

➤ What are the positive and negative consequences of what you did?

➤ What are the potential obstacles that will occur with your solution?

These questions address the issue and give people a chance to fully explain themselves and express their positions.

The Benefits of Asking Powerful Questions

Powerful questions will help you learn both about the person you're speaking with and the subject you're discussing. You can find out how the person thinks and what is important to them, based upon what they say and don't say. The more you continue to ask powerful questions, the more you will accomplish both. This confirms George Bernard Shaw's point: "The problem with communication is the illusion that it has been accomplished." So often we fall into a trap in which we believe we understand each other and grasp the concepts being explained, only to later find that it was almost as if we were speaking a different language to one another. Continual probing and on-target questions will help both you and the other person arrive at the best solution, and learn more about each other and yourselves.

It seems obvious since we spent two chapters discussing the importance of listening, but when a question is asked, allow the other person the time to respond. You want to be sure that thought processing and critical thinking are at play. I had one client who felt that the reason the respondent didn't answer immediately was that he or she didn't have an answer. If you want a quick answer, there is a really low probability that you will gain a truly thoughtful answer. If your expectation from a thought-provoking question is a quick answer, you risk the other person being frustrated in a nonproductive way, with you and with themselves.

Powerful questions also satiate your sense of curiosity. *When you are curious, you want to learn more and you will more naturally ask questions in ways that will maximize the other person's thinking.* When the right question does not come to mind or the person was not clear in what he or she said or was trying to say, you can always respond: "Tell me more about that." This simple phrase will expand the other person's thinking as they further verbalize their thoughts and your understanding of what they are saying. When one is not naturally curious, the desire to respect the other person by exploring their thinking provides a solid motivation to ask questions that bring out the person's best thinking. Instead of saying, "Stay thirsty, my friend," as Jonathan Goldsmith did in the Dos Equis ads, say to yourself, "Stay curious, my friend." Lack of curiosity can be the foe of getting to the best result.

> **When you are curious, you want to learn more and you will more naturally ask questions in ways that will maximize the other person's thinking.**

Powerful questions are perfect for discussing sensitive matters. Asking difficult, tough, or edgy questions can be hard for even the most veteran leaders, but those who want their colleagues and team members to succeed will of course need to ask some from time to time. As a coach, I ask those questions fairly often to bring out my client's very best thinking. When the person is asked a tough question that reflects on them personally, you will find it interesting, maybe surprising, and rewarding to first ask for their permission to ask a difficult question. The typical question is simply something like: "May I ask you a tough question about all of this?" (This is one example of when a yes/no question is wise.)

Tough or difficult questions are direct and go to the heart of personal accountability and, at the same time can inspire a higher level of performance. Examples of such questions include: "In retrospect, what could you have done differently to create the outcome we wanted?" or "What was an even better way for you to handle that?" These questions will help them reflect on their decisions and actions, and also on what they can do in the future to improve. A question such as, "What do you need to do to greatly improve this situation?" or "What specifically will you commit to do differently when this or a similar situation arises?" may feel too pointed at first, but it will lead to them being more reflective and thoughtful, help them avoid the same actions in the future, and to grow as a leader. These kinds of pointed questions also demonstrate that you care about them as a person and you care about their success—and they reflect clearly on who is responsible. They have no sense of "gotcha," which tends to make it about you more than their responsibility.

One powerful way to inspire others is ask questions that touch the core of who a person is or who they want to be as a both a person and as a leader. Those types of questions tend to strengthen the foundation of who someone is or wants to be. They signal a respect for that person and a sense of keen interest in them. In giving that signal, what do you think their view of you as someone they want to follow will be? Some examples of such questions are: "In what ways did your actions reflect on who you want to be as a leader?," "What should you change to create a better result next time?," and "What do you think should be or are the consequences of what you did (or the consequences of what happened)?" The last question, of course, asks the person to say out loud what the consequences are for them and for the business. In some ways when they say it, it has a greater impact on them than if you do—especially when you affirm to them those are the consequences. In that situation, it might also be wise if they left an important consequence unsaid to ask: "What are some other consequences?" or "What about . . . ?" Another question to improve self-awareness and future performance is: "Taking a fresh look at this, which of your talents can you use to improve on what you did or said?"

Powerful questions also help remove distracting emotions or prevent traveling on rabbit trails from the conversation. The questions will often start with asking for a description of the forest—the broader view. This helps the other person get out of the woods and out of their own way. This is particularly the case when the other person is buried in the complexities and minutia of a certain situation. Some examples of questions to help someone extract their mind from the nonessential details and emotional reactions are:

> ➤ As you look at the bigger picture, what are the key things in play here?

> ➤ If you selected one or two things that are most important to accomplish, what would they be?

➤ What really matters to you?

➤ What really matters to the person or group most affected?

➤ What will cause this effort to actually work?

➤ What will motivate the players involved to take positive and productive action?

➤ What makes a specific person or position critical in our company?

➤ What do you think is at the heart of this issue?

➤ Where should your focus be?

➤ What are the things you can do that are most important for your success?

➤ What are the benefits if you focus more on the most important things you just identified?

Powerful questions are the only ones that will get the conversation to where it should go, providing solutions and helping everyone involved move forward with increased vigor and excitement about the current task or project. Let's look at an example from a client I worked with that helped her colleague overcome a barrier through the use of powerful questions.

Powerful Questions in Action

The following discussion took place between my client, Jane, the CFO at a very large manufacturing company, and Sally, the corporate controller. Sally had a problem with a direct report, George, the director of acquisition analysis, who seemed to be taking a lackadaisical approach to a time-sensitive project. George is a brilliant analyst and puts on a good front of being a good old fellow who is laid back. Sally was clearly frustrated by what she perceived as George's lack of urgency, and Jane responded with powerful questions to help Sally create questions that would lead and inspire George:

Sally: I am having a really hard time understanding why George does not see the urgency to finish the project he has (the acquisition of an innovative company in an industry that is not known for its innovation).

Jane: Tell me about the urgency.

Sally: The project George has, if he finishes it on time, will allow us to beat our competition into the market with a new product.

Jane: What do you think you can do to help him understand the urgency?

Sally: He is a smart guy, so it is especially frustrating that he does not seem to get that this is critical.

Jane: That is frustrating. What can you do to help him better understand the urgency?

Sally: I suppose I can talk to him about it again.

Jane: What is the best question to ask him?

Sally: George, I don't get it. Why don't you understand the urgency?

Jane: What do you think his reaction will be if you ask it that way?

Sally: Well, as I think about it, I think he would be defensive and think I do not believe he is smart enough to get it.

Jane: What would be a better way to ask the question to get his best thinking on the subject?

Sally: George, what are the reasons your project has great urgency?

Jane: What do you think asking it that way will accomplish?

Sally: He will not feel defensive. He will have to articulate why it does have a sense of urgency. It will be his thoughts and not mine. I will have the opportunity to ask follow-up questions if needed. Because the question was open-ended and did not reveal any of my thoughts about the subject, I will have a better opportunity to hear his.

Jane: When would be the best time to talk with George?

Sally: I will do it tomorrow morning.

Jane: Good. I'll look forward to hearing how it goes.

In this exchange, Jane demonstrated respect for Sally—and for George. She was able to help Sally come to a solution but not lead her with her own thoughts on the issue. Jane let Sally determine the best way to understand George and help George to understand the urgency of the project, and she did so only through the powerful questions she raised. Notice that Jane avoided the "whys," and by doing so immediately helped Sally resolve the issue. She also helped Sally understand that "what" questions would be better in finding a solution, keeping George from feeling defensive, and allowing their thinking to not be bound by limitations.

By focusing on executing a decision, neither partici-pant became distracted by inconsequential information or issues. Jane did this by first affirming to Sally that the situation was frustrating but then removed Sally's emotion and frustration from the picture. She helped Sally think through the next step and caused her to articulate what made it the best action to move forward. She also gave Sally time, using silence to form her best thoughts, and boosted her confidence in her ability to solve the issue. All of this was accomplished in only two and a half minutes!

> **Repetition shows the importance of the question and gives the other person permission to think more deeply about what they think is the best response.**

The Jane/Sally/George example, in its brevity and simplicity, demonstrates how questions can bring out another person's best thinking. One of the keys is to keep asking "what" questions. As you read in the example, Jane was not afraid to repeat the exact same question. I do that in my coaching. Repetition shows the importance of the question and gives the other person permission to think more deeply about what they think is the best response.

Sample Questions Used to Reach Specific Goals

Open discourse, the process of listening and asking questions, is the foundation upon which success can be built, but it is difficult for many of us. Powerful questions contribute to positive discussions and lead to superior results. Still, they can be hard to develop. The best way to begin using them is by practicing them every day. To get you started, try asking the following questions. Keep in mind that you can also ask yourself powerful questions to clear your mind and move forward.

Questions to create high expectations and inspire

➤ I am curious: What were the most important things you did to cause this project to be so successful?

➤ What are the highest expectations you have for yourself?

➤ What would you be thinking if your confidence was even higher than it is now?

➤ What is your very best thinking related to this topic?

➤ What are the things you could do to more fully capitalize on your strengths?

➤ What are you doing that makes you most pleased with the work you are performing?

➤ What can *you* do to make this project succeed?

➤ If you want to "go for the gold," what is the "gold" for you?

➤ What brings you the most delight (or satisfaction or fulfillment) in your work?

To get unstuck in one's thinking

➤ What is the most important thing you need to be thinking about related to this dilemma?

➤ If you put this problem/challenge in its most simple and direct terms, how would you describe it?

➤ Going beyond the superficial, what do we really want to accomplish here?

➤ What is at the heart of this issue or problem?

➤ If you were to take just the first step to solving this problem or challenge, what would it be?

➤ What is the first thing you should be thinking and doing about this issue?

➤ What troubles you most about this challenge?

To generate thinking geared toward best thinking and positive action

➤ If you were to think creatively about this situation, what comes to mind?

➤ What has never been done or tried before that might actually work in this situation?

➤ What is the best course of action?

➤ What makes that solution the very best one?

➤ Who, based on their experience and their talents, do you believe should be a part of creating the very best thinking and solutions?

➤ What is your sense of the urgency in getting this done, solving this problem, or getting the results we need?

➤ What else do we need to know about this opportunity?

➤ Based on that information and the other factors we've considered, what conclusions can you draw?

➤ What does the elephant in this room look like?

➤ Keeping in mind our mission and values, what are the most important aspects of this approach?

On-boarding new employees

To the team members of the team the new person will be joining:

➤ What do we need to do to create the foundation upon which the new team member can build his or her success?

➤ What are your best ideas around accelerating a smooth and rapid integration of the new person into our culture and team?

➤ What relationships are key to the early performance of the new person?

➤ What can we do to facilitate those relationships?

➤ What would each of you like to commit to do to execute these ideas?

To ask the new person:

➤ What will be the most important things your teammates can do to help to integrate you into your new team?

➤ What questions do you have about our culture and personal characteristics that are helpful in becoming an integral part of your new team?

➤ What are the best things we can do to help you achieve your goals?

➤ What do you believe you need to do to have a smooth and positive transition?

To achieve better self-evaluation

➤ What is most important to me in terms of what I want to accomplish or lead others to accomplish?

➤ What am I doing that is really smart based on what I want to accomplish?

➤ What seems to be driving my success?

➤ What are my talents?

➤ As I honestly look at myself and the direct and indirect messages I have received from others, what should I be doing differently and better?

➤ What must I do to more fully use my talents?

➤ What am I doing that someone else should be doing?

➤ Who do I want to be as a person? As a leader?

➤ In what ways are my words and actions in sync with who I want to be as a person and as a leader?

Powerful Questions Make You the Best You Can Be

Powerful questions help people better understand their environment and the situation they're facing, which leads to creating and verbalizing the best possible solutions. As they have the opportunity to think through what is important to them, they are able to explain what motivates them, leading them toward a plan of what needs to be done. Powerful questions work through and beyond the quagmire of the complexity of many challenges *and allow us to formulate an action plan.* They help to articulate the problem, advocate a solution, and lead toward the desired results.

In doing so, they provide direction and new ways of thinking. The response "I have not thought about that" is one of the best you can receive from your questions. You're giving the other person the opportunity to think about new solutions in a positive way. You also show respect for the person who is being asked the question. When you genuinely want to know what the other person thinks, you signal your respect for them and they recognize it. Powerful questions inspire these people and help them achieve their highest level of thinking and creativity. You are able to more easily develop positive relationships and create strong advocates for the desired course of action. When a person is able to articulate their reasoned thinking and solution, it is most likely the best solution. They become effective advocates who can explain the plan or sell it to others. Their confidence grows as you help them arrive at the best solution and action plan and they come away thinking, "Hey, I solved that problem; I am pretty smart." In turn, they appreciate you.

Dr. Seuss said, "Sometimes the questions are complicated and the answers are simple." Turn that around: Ask simple and direct questions and then listen to what thinking emerges. Make your questions create greater clarity and simplicity. Powerful questions clear the fog and provide the light needed to develop others' best thinking and inspire their confidence to soar. Using key questions at the right time, in the correct context, and in a positive way cause both your team and you individually to achieve more on a regular basis. When armed with powerful questions and the willingness and ability to listen to the answers, you'll be able to develop an action plan to move forward toward success—the topic of our next chapter.

4

Develop Others' Best Thinking

It is only as we develop others that we permanently succeed.
—Henry Firestone

My client, Thomas, who truly knows his business and was acknowledged for his intelligence, gained great satisfaction from having the answers to many of the challenges, large and small, his company faced. He also relished giving his followers the answers to their questions and solving problems for which they were responsible. All of his direct reports depended on him to solve their challenges and he thoroughly enjoyed doing so. It was stimulating for him. It was gratifying. He found, however, that he was growing increasingly frustrated with the performance of the organization.

As Thomas responded to my questions about his leadership style, he began to have a greater self-awareness of the effect of being the one person who had most of the answers and solutions. Because he was *the* guy, his followers relied on him, rather than on themselves to find the answers to their issues. It was time consuming for him; it limited individual growth of his reports and negatively affected his team and the entire organization. As a result of his openness to some probing questions, he started to understand the negative impact he was having on his company. He became determined to make a substantial change in his leadership style and commit himself to listen and ask questions, and require his followers to think through the best possible solutions.

Like any lifelong habit, it was difficult for him to refrain from giving "the answer" and, through the questions asked, bring out the other person's best thinking. He used his talents of tenacity, self-discipline, and the resolve to stifle his own sense of achievement and satisfaction that came from having the answers—from being the "smartest one." The most significant results were not immediate, but throughout the next six to nine months the culture did shift. The performance metrics improved and Thomas attributed the improvement to one key change:

The evolution of the culture to one in which leaders, through the questions they asked, now required their direct reports to create their *own* solutions. This dramatic improvement only happened as a result of Thomas's discipline and focus to alter a fundamental part of his leadership style. He understood what would be gained and had the resolve to make the difficult change. Thomas also gained as much personal satisfaction from bringing out the best thinking of others as he did demonstrating his own intelligence. It was a change that had a significant impact on him personally and on his entire leadership team.

Great listening leads to great questions. Great questions yield great thinking. *Great thinking leads to great solutions.* Great solutions lead to higher performance and people inspired to achieve their best. The idea is to help others go from "I don't get it" to "I got it!" "I now think I have the best solution, the timeline, and the ability to lead the execution of the plan." You will, as a result of your questions, guide them to expand their thinking and achieve what you believe is the best solution and timeline.

Ronald Reagan was quoted as saying, "The greatest leader is not necessarily the one who does the greatest things. He is the one that gets the people to do the greatest things." By helping others grow, you give them the opportunity to take ownership of their actions and the results. You are in a leadership role to bring out the best in everyone, to facilitate solutions and inspire. To develop an action plan, think—in some depth—about what it is you want to accomplish; ask questions; take a step back so they can see the bigger picture and help others find the solution on their own, using your questions to inspire them.

Help Others Develop and Execute Their Plans

With few exceptions, all of the executive leaders who I have coached believe that their accomplishments are, in substantial part, attributed to their ability to create the solutions for challenges as they arise. Consciously or subconsciously, just like my client Thomas, part of their fulfillment comes from being the smartest person in the room, the one with all the answers. They want to be the brightest, and in charge, and have that fact apparent to all. There is nothing inherently wrong about that natural desire. It does, however, have the effect of limiting followers' growth and their ability to implement solutions in ways that may not have been considered.

> "A leader's job is not to do the work for others, it's to help others figure out how to do it themselves, to get things done, and to succeed beyond what they thought possible."
> —Simon Sinek

When you encourage others' best thinking, and allow them through your questions to achieve their best thinking and solutions, you demonstrate that you value and respect them. If they feel that you are not supporting them or valuing their abilities, their confidence will lessen and they will be timid in their approaches to execute the plans you or someone else created. By reducing their responsibility for creating their own solutions, you diminish their willingness to take risks or initiative, and the opportunities for their career growth are diminished. You stifle their ability to think through what the best solutions are, which means they don't learn the critical thinking skills necessary to solve issues. In effect, you limit their best possible thought process, which also limits the thought processes of everyone else involved, including your own, making your life as a leader more demanding than it needs to be.

Think of a time when you had a boss who relished having all the answers and who never sincerely sought out your best thinking. What was your sense of value to your boss, to the organization? How did you feel about your contribution and how did it affect your performance? What impact did it have on your career? Did you feel stifled?

When a leader requires others to think through and develop their own solutions and action plans, performance soars. As a leader, you are helping develop the other person's best and brightest thinking. The best solution and action plan are found through a combination of their thoughts and your questions. This is not to suggest that you become disengaged from the situation. In fact, your involvement is at a high level. Your discussion becomes a partnership in reaching the best plan. You ask questions and the other person is challenged and inspired to expand his or her thinking.

When you inspire someone to be thorough in their thinking and develop their own solutions, you not only give them the knowledge and courage to execute the current plan and achieve the needed outcomes, but you also help them develop and grow as a stronger and clearer thinker—and as a much more successful leader. In the process, you give them ownership of the process and results/success that is achieved. You inspire them to possibly exceed your and their expectations. When they own it, they have an extra stake in the game. They have an additional dose of personal pride and motivation for it to succeed. They don't simply think, "Well the boss told me to do this." Through your questions, you articulate what makes their solution or plan the best one and therefore effectively communicate the plan to others with clarity. It is their plan; no one else's.

By helping them develop the plan, instead of telling them what to do and maybe even how to do it, you demonstrate your respect for the members of your team and your other colleagues.

Spending more time listening and asking direct, penetrating questions does in fact save time later because there are fewer re-dos and greater clarity and accountability.

This point rarely occurs to any of the leaders I coach. When I mention it, however, they do "get" the notion quickly and it becomes a substantial motivator to make the change. Leaders also find that when they are willing to trust others, they not only show their respect, but they also give themselves more time to provide their fullest value to the organization. You will have more time to do the things that you are paid to do and that create the greatest value for the organization and for you.

Overcome Assumptions

It is easy to assume that helping others to develop their own solutions will take too much of your time. Many leaders believe it is much easier and faster just to tell the person what to do, but this is most often true only in the short term. If the person owns the solution and the plan, that is a powerful force in getting the work done well and on time. And that will save *you* a substantial amount of time. Every leader whom I have coached has discovered that initially spending a bit more time listening and asking direct, penetrating questions does in fact save time later on when it comes to successfully executing the plan. Another assumption many of my clients have is that if the people working for them were smart enough to figure out the current problem, then they would have already found the right answer. They would not be coming to their boss for the solution. If you are the boss and your subordinates have been coming to you for the solutions to all of their problems, it is logical for them to think that they should be providing all the answers to the people they lead as well.

When you require the person to create their own solutions, however, you can play a key role in forming the plan and still let the other person own it by asking thoughtful questions as needed to direct their thinking. To illustrate this idea, here is a factual representation based on an experience I had with a client.

A president of a large organization, Bob, was struggling with having enough time to do the things that should have been priorities. Rather, he found that he was performing other people's work, which took him away from completing the tasks integral to his job. You will see in this exchange how asking simple and direct questions inspires followers to own their decisions and take action. The exchange also naturally flows into a discussion related to delegation and accountability.

In most conversations such as this one, it is most effective to move directly to the issue, placing the responsibility squarely on the person who wants to make changes in their ability to develop solutions and execute on them.

I asked, "What changes do you think you need to make to give yourself more time?"

Bob took a moment to consider, then told me: "I really don't know. I have thought about it and haven't come up with any answers. I do know that I am working too many hours and the performance of the organization is not what I want it to be."

Since he was stuck, I prompted his thinking by asking him to start with just one thought: "If you were to think of one thing you might do differently, what would it be? "

"Well," he said, "when one of my direct reports does not complete a project or is struggling with it, I tend to do it for him. It just seems easier and quicker."

I wanted him to consider what was in the best interest for the other person, so I asked, "What is the consequence for them when that happens?"

Again, Bob took a moment and was silent, but then said, "They have no sense of being accountable, which brings up another concern I have. The culture of this company does not seem to consistently include everyone being accountable for what they commit to do."

Though his answer seemed somewhat loaded, I wanted to make sure that he realized I wasn't judging his response or him. I asked, "Based on what you have just said, what role do you play in creating the culture?" I said it in this direct and clear way to help him create greater self-awareness. In doing so, he had to honestly assess the situation.

He candidly told me, "I am not only allowing the culture to persist, but demonstrating how it works!" This was a valuable insight, and I told him so, which gave him direct affirmation and emphasized his new sense of self-awareness.

From there, I wanted to return to the main problem. I said, "Getting back to you spending less time at work and having more time to do the things that produce the greatest of results for the company, what else can you do to free up more time?" This comes back to the target and slightly reframes the issue while asking for deeper thinking.

After another pause, he said, "I will work on holding others consistently accountable and will try to stop doing the work others should be doing. That will save me considerable time."

Affirming his statement and moving toward his accountability and measurement of success, I said, "That is great." Then I asked, "What are the best ways for you to measure your success in accomplishing that goal?"

"I will need to really focus on it." he told me. "It will be hard to break that habit as that is what I have been doing for years. The best way to measure it for me will be to keep a simple log of the number of times I slip up and offer to do what one of my subordinates has committed to do."

I highly recommend that leaders keep logs on their progress. It helps to focus their thoughts and see how they've improved. It can be hard to keep up with the logs. So, I wanted to help Bob think through his commitment and eliminate reasons for not being accountable. I asked, "What will be the most difficult aspect of keeping the log?"

"Just remembering it and doing it concurrently with the event," Bob said.

This question helped him to think more about this, but I wanted him to consider it further. It's important to force people to think through how this can work best for them and gives them a more positive outlook for achieving the goal. I asked, "What will make it easier for you?"

"I keep a journal in front of me during all meetings," he told me. "I will write on the top of the page DSEW, which means 'did someone else's work' and put a tick mark when I do that."

"That sounds simple and effective. What else can you do differently to save more time?" I asked, to affirm his thinking and to encourage him to dig even deeper for the most complete solution. "As we've been talking, I was also thinking that I could do a better job delegating."

At this point, I wanted to open up the conversation more, allowing for the most thoughtful answers possible. I told him to share more of his thinking about delegation with me.

"Honestly," he said, "I have a tendency to hang on to the things I have always enjoyed doing, like reviewing the financials in great detail. I do that because I like to know how we are doing and the best way to do that is to dig into the weeds. I have a great CFO who could do that for me, and frankly maybe she'd do it even better. I also have an operations background and know my COO is slammed with work, so I am hesitant to give him the work I probably should. I do it myself rather than delegating to him. He has a young family and I worry that he should spend more time with them."

Bob gave me a lot to work with in that statement, so I wanted to help him think through and articulate the barriers that he was creating. "So, what are the key reasons you do not delegate as much as you could?" I asked.

Again, silence. Then, he said, "The two things I just mentioned—I harken back to what I used to do and do it well, so I enjoy doing it, and I feel sorry for those who are spending too much time at work."

I asked, "What do you need to do to change the way you think about delegating? "As with all the questions, there is no personal judgment here, just a drive to reach the best solution. The question is direct and on target.

Bob replied, "Now that it is clearer that I need to delegate more, I need to think about what will motivate me to change."

"Looking at possible motivating factors," I responded, "in what ways does you holding others consistently accountable and delegating effectively show that you respect them?" This question requires him to think about a new way to consider the benefits of delegating and holding them accountable. Whenever I ask similar questions of my clients, they typically begin to think of new motivating factors that will help them make the desired changes.

In this instance, Bob said, "I never thought about that." Silence. "It does show that I trust them, which is a key pillar of respecting another person." Silence. "As you have caused me to think more about this, I also realize that holding others consistently accountable and delegating wisely helps give my people confidence and the experience they need to achieve more and reach higher goals."

It was important for him to realize this fact and I wanted to keep the focus on him. This discussion was all about Bob's thinking and what will work best for him in making the changes that will lead to actionable results. I asked him, "What makes that important to you?"

"It is important to me that I respect others and show confidence in them. And now it occurs to me that delegating more to them and holding them accountable will accomplish both those things."

To signal I was listening and emphasize the point, I said: "It will show you respect them and have confidence in them." I then followed it up with a positive question to help him think through the best reasons for him to effectively and wisely delegate. "What effect will you delegating more have on your direct reports and how they in turn delegate tasks?"

"I know they do look at how I lead, so maybe it will get the point across that they need to delegate more effectively as well."

It was obvious he was starting to get it, and we were moving toward the action plan, but I wanted to broaden his sense of purpose, so I asked what else he could do to help imbed the concept of more effective delegation into the company's culture.

He said, "It does make sense to tell them I am going to be delegating more to them and tell them why."

Always coming back to measuring success, I asked, "What will be the best way for you to measure your success in delegating more wisely?"

He returned to the tool we had discussed. "I can use a log to easily keep track of how many times I delegated something I might have previously done myself and, with the help of my assistant, we will measure how much more time I have available. My goal will be to use that time to block out periods to think, to catch up with the hundreds of emails I get daily, and to do more of the things I think take best advantage of my talents for those with whom I work and the company."

"Those goals make a lot of sense," I said and added, "What do you see as the other benefits of making these changes?" By making this statement and raising this question, my intention was to create a clear awareness of what would motivate Bob to make this difficult change.

"Substantial," he replied. "I will have more time and, equally important, this is a good way to start changing the culture of the company to one in which accountability becomes a hallmark."

"So, what is your level of optimism now for having more time available?"

"I have clarified my thinking and have new insights of awareness that will motivate me. So, it is high." A good response! I wanted to further help him maintain a sustainable focus and a sense of clarity, so I asked him to recap his plan to give himself more time.

"It is simple to say and tough to do," he told me. "I will hold others more consistently accountable and I will delegate more, especially those things that I enjoy doing, but are not really the most valuable use of my time." Here he is doubling down on his action plan, but I wanted to make sure he kept in mind that this was all in an attempt to create results, so I again emphasized measuring them.

"What are the best measures of your success?" I asked.

"The easiest is seeing how much time I save. But, because we are now talking about not just saving time but changing the culture, I should measure the number of times I am successful in helping others develop their own action plans and then allow them to own the accountability for getting it accomplished on time."

I asked, "What is the best way for you to keep track of *your* success?" This was another directed yet open question for Bob to arrive at his own way to measure his accomplishments.

He repeated, "I will carry a tick sheet on a note card and keep track of it as I go along," he suggested.

It seemed that Bob now had a clear sense of what he wanted to do and that he was directly responsible for doing it. As his coach, he knew that I would be available to support him. If you use this leadership approach, your followers will know that you will support them and hold them accountable. What would be the practical benefit for you, the reader, if you would regularly take this approach when helping employees, team members, or colleagues in developing an action plan? I asked him directly, "What is the best way for me to help you be accountable for doing that?" He told me he would give me a detailed progress report in two weeks. This approach worked well as it set a timetable and motivated him to get it done—to be accountable.

"Great," I told him. "I think you have the will and the tenacity to give yourself more time and it sounds like it may have a profound effect on the culture and performance of the company." In saying this, his plan was affirmed and his efforts encouraged, creating a higher probability of success. I also asked if he wanted to recap in writing his thoughts coming out of our discussion and then send them to me. Crystallizing and writing down one's new thoughts, what they heard, and the commitments they made has been an important element in helping my clients achieve their goals. He was happy to take me up on my offer and said, "I am relieved and energized, and ready to take action on my commitment."

Clients who start asking their subordinates to send them a note highlighting what they learned from the discussion, what they will commit to do, and when they'll do it, have reported that just doing that has had a substantial impact. It has:

> Crystallized the other person's thinking.

> Caused them to think even more clearly about the issues/opportunities discussed.

> Made the accountabilities and timeline clearer.

At first it may seem awkward or off-putting to ask for a recap. However, if you do, you and your subordinates will quickly see the benefits. Asking for a recap of the most important things they heard and the commitments they made is especially impactful and motivating when they know in advance you will be asking them to do that.

Prior to this exchange, Bob had not thought about and verbalized the changes needed to more successfully manage his time. As Bob thought through the ways he could save time, he actually started considering the culture of the organization and his role in promulgating a culture he said he wanted to change. What seemed like a fairly narrow subject—sticking to and making time to achieve the goals for which he was personally responsible (time management)—turned into ideas to change the entire organization's culture. This kind of expansion of thinking occurs often in coaching and can happen to you as a leader when you ask great questions and inspire the best thinking of your followers.

A relatively short discussion (approximately four minutes) yielded a plan of action for him and started him working on the plan. Bob created his own solutions and action plan with questions designed to help him expand and clarify his thinking and gain new insights. You will find that when developing an action plan, the follower's direct challenge will begin to be resolved and your questions will lead to dealing with larger, or in some cases, underlying issues. When the issue is raised and discussed and then an action plan created, it often is the case that the original issue is at the heart of a broader challenge.

Forward Thinking

How many meetings have you been in or even led in which the discussion focused on what went wrong? This is part of a coaching exchange with Joel, a CEO client. Joel said in a meeting with his direct reports, "We did not make our revenue goal of $100 million for the quarter. We were $7 million short. What happened? How did we screw up?" As he reflected on the outcome of that meeting, Joel said, "There was a frank discussion of who did not do what was needed, what should have been more closely controlled, and what was beyond our control. At the end of that meeting most believed that they had failed and clearly needed to do better. But as I think about it, no one was clear on what it was specifically that should be done differently. We agreed that we would continue to forge a plan to meet the revenue targets in our next meeting." I asked Joel to think about focusing on what each person will commit to do differently to achieve their revenue goal.

Joel said during our next coaching exchange that he tried focusing just on *forward thinking*. He told his team:

> We all know we were $7 million short of making our $100 million revenue goal. We talked

last meeting about what went wrong. Now let's focus on what we need to do differently and in what ways we need to be smarter to get back on track. As I said in my email to you, we are going to start with each of us giving our best thinking about one thing we will commit to do differently to directly or indirectly increase revenue. I will start by asking my assistant to reconstruct from my calendar how many hours I spent with key customers and commit to spending four more hours a month with them. I'll ask my assistant to keep track of my hours. I will also review with Sally (the chief Marketing Officer) what we want to accomplish in each customer meeting and the best strategy to achieve it. The rest of the team put forth the key thing they will commit to do differently and better to increase revenues. After that meeting my team seemed to be inspired and to have a clearer sense of exactly what needs to be done. Since everyone, even those with no direct responsibility for revenue, committed to a specific action, there was a heightened sense that this a real team effort. Everyone sent me a note after the meeting with a clear statement of what they committed to do and their timeline. As I look back on it, the meeting about what went wrong had little or no positive effect on reaching our revenue goal. Next time we will focus from the get go on what we need to do and who will do it.

When leaders focus on what can be done, people are inspired to achieve more, especially when they think of and articulate what it is that they are going to do.

People Are Smart

It has become clear through my observation of hundreds of executives and through my coaching that incredible results can come when the leader asks powerful questions that bring out a subordinate's best thinking. There is a caution here. People are smart. If your intention is to guide a person to your way of thinking or the solution you know to be the best, others will realize that fact. They then might easily think: "I just wish he'd tell me what to do or think and get on with it" or "Why does she go through with this charade rather just telling me what to do?" Leaders who are genuine always achieve greater respect, loyalty, and results than those who are not. If your intention is to have them do exactly what you know to be best, avoid leading them to your answer or solution. Rather, gain their greater understanding and buy-in by asking something like: "What do you see as the advantages of doing it (the way you know to be best)?" In that way, they are required to think through, as you did, what exactly makes this the best solution. If they miss a key element ask questions like: "What are your thoughts about (the piece they missed)?" The goal is for them to articulate what makes the plan the best rather than you telling them. *And*, it takes surprisingly little time while bringing a clarity that sticks in their minds.

5

The Art of Acknowledging and Inspiring

One of the best ways to inspire a leader to achieve great success is to tell him or her what they have done especially well so that they are energized to repeat what they did. If you are a keen observer (i.e., you pay attention), there will be many opportunities to do exactly that.

Andy Pearson was a McKinsey managing director, president and Chief Operating Officer at PepsiCo for fifteen years, a Harvard Business School professor, and the founding CEO and chairman of Yum Brands. (Tricon Global was the restaurant business owned by PepsiCo and, after it was spun off, it became Yum Brands—

one of the world's largest restaurant companies.) At PepsiCo, before Yum Brands, Pearson was known as a leader who inspired others through fear and intimidation. He had a well-earned reputation as an abrasive leader who belittled people, invoked fear, and intimidated and paralyzed people with his command of the numbers and his unrelenting demand for more from his subordinate leaders.

As CEO of Yum Brands, however, Pearson transformed himself and his leadership style. He became a leader who inspired his followers to want to achieve success *because* of him, instead of in spite of him.

Andy transformed the core characteristics of his leadership at age 76. Though he had been quite effective for the prior fifty years, he dramatically changed his thoughts and actions related to leading others. Andy is certainly a model for the idea that it is never too late or too difficult to change how you lead. With a passion for continuing to become the best leader you can be, substantial change is possible at any age! Although Andy's transformation was extraordinary, it illustrates that we all have opportunities for change whether they are incremental or dramatic. So, if you are in your forties, fifties, or sixties, take heart and realize you *can* make dramatic changes in your leadership behavior.

Andy realized that in order to create loyal, sustainable leadership teams and employees, there are tremendous advantages to reach the heart—from which one is motivated in extraordinary ways. He recognized that responding to the need for acknowledgment and approval is a powerful way to gain the highest level of thinking and performance from people. He also learned that people who feel respected are capable of so much more than he, or they, may have initially thought.

> **"Outstanding leaders appeal to the hearts
> of their followers, not their minds."**
> **—Unknown**

Pearson began motivating his followers by acknowledging the things they did well. He now believes that it's less important to issue orders than it is to seek answers and ideas from others. He sees that his job is to listen to the people who work for him and to serve them. The "old fashion" leadership style of telling them what to do and expecting them to do it because you are the boss will not cut it with millennials and it will not gain the level of success needed for anyone, in any organization.

What would it be like if all the people you work with recognized you as an inspiring leader? What changes can you make to become that inspiring leader?

It is easy in the world of a results-oriented business to miss one of the most powerful ways to achieve those results: *through inspired employees*. Employees who value and trust you will naturally be more productive and better equipped to create the results you want. When you show respect for others, you signal your high expectations for them and they naturally want to meet those expectations. There are many ways to inspire others. Some use fear— fear of losing one's job, that is. Others do it through their powerful use of words, emotion, and ability to persuade. Other leaders act as an example of the behavior they wish their team to emulate. And others do so by skillfully acknowledging the other person's talent, what they said, and what they accomplished. Most inspire others using a combination of skills.

I believe in the power of acknowledgment as an extraordinarily effective way to inspire others. Acknowledgments that are specific and genuine will affect others beyond what you might have thought possible. As I coach senior executives who are working to evolve into more inspirational leaders, they become more aware of the power of genuine acknowledgments and the need to develop this skill and use it effectively. Before they can begin doing so, however, they first need to understand what is meant by "acknowledgment."

Acknowledgment Versus Compliments

In order to inspire others through acknowledgment, it is first helpful to recognize the *difference between giving compliments and giving genuine acknowledgments*. One of my senior-level clients told me that his employees do not need compliments and he is not comfortable giving them. "Compliments should be restricted to a social environment," he once told me. When I explained to him the distinct difference between a compliment and an acknowledgment he began to think more positively about the value of an acknowledgment.

A *compliment* is a casual and positive recognition. Compliments give the recipient a sense of feeling good, especially if you give the compliment that you believe is honest. For example, a compliment such as "You did a good job!" or "You are smart!" make people feel positive, happy, and comfortable. Similarly, a compliment can refer to an external factor, such as someone's style. Telling a person that they have a great looking tie, dress, suit, shirt, or pair of shoes can result in a nice, feel-good style of communication. Compliments are at the surface level and don't have the motivational impact that acknowledgments do.

An *acknowledgment* is a genuine and factual recognition of what someone did including a specific detail related to the action the person has performed. It is direct and best received with no fluff or puff. When you acknowledge someone, you are calling attention to a specific behavior or talent, and it comes without any type of extra modifiers. By this I mean that an acknowledgment stands alone without qualifiers that could diminish it. The power comes from your taking the time and making the effort to note some specific positive action or talent of another person and reporting your observation to them. An acknowledgment also inspires the recipient to repeat that behavior or action. I think of a compliment as being skin deep and a genuine acknowledgment reaching one's soul. That may sound dramatic, yet, when you start giving others clear acknowledgments you will see, over time, the tremendously positive effect they have.

Give an Acknowledgment

An acknowledgment requires you to observe and report on what another person has done. It requires your attention to the people around you and their accomplishments. You must first carefully observe what the person said or did. That fact is what gives an acknowledgment its value to the recipients, as they will be appreciative that you noticed their actions and achievements. The leaders with whom I have worked have found it easier to be more aware of opportunities to acknowledge others when they think of themselves as observant reporters. The leader observes with some level of detail and perception what a person did well and reports that to the person. If you struggle with giving acknowledgments, one approach to make acknowledgments easier for you to give is to make a list of the attributes or abilities that are most important to you. Then use those factors to help you notice when others exhibit them. With the positive insight, your followers are inspired to continue to use those noted talents and behaviors.

It is important to note that acknowledging someone is not just some nice thing to do! *An acknowledgment reaches deeper into a person's heart and mind and lifts them up with the courage and the knowledge to continue the desired behaviors.* Acknowledgments may have been rare in your life, but think of one time someone you respected acknowledged something you did. In what ways did that inspire you? This may also bring to mind how rare genuine acknowledgments are and therefore the impact they can have.

Genuine and sincere acknowledgments lead a person to respect and trust you more. And when someone feels that way about you, he or she is more likely to be inspired by you as well. All of us have noticed but may not have thought much about this idea. When someone expresses honest and specific appreciation for something we have done or accomplished, we value them more, even though we may not have thought about why that is. This happens because that person took the time and energy to notice something that is important and specific to us—and cared enough—to acknowledge and encourage us.

If you choose to acknowledge others, you will begin to see the impact in a relatively short period of time. The more genuine acknowledgments one receives, the more he or she will be able, motivated, and inspired to think clearly and act decisively. *Genuine* is emphasized because that makes each acknowledgment authentic and powerful. Genuine acknowledgments can be given spontaneously or with some pre-thought and one does not need to worry about giving them too frequently because they are always sincere and based on your factual observations. Also, they are given with no fluff or puff.

Inspire Through Acknowledgments

Your ability as a leader to inspire others through acknowledgments really boils down to just two things that everyone has the capability of doing: notice others' unusual accomplishments and specifically what they did to achieve those accomplishments, and then report to that person what you have observed without any qualifiers, "buts," or fluff. Author and leadership and management expert Ken Blanchard put it simply when he stated: "Exemplary leaders personalize recognition. They catch what people do right."[1]

It is helpful to understand and internalize the fact that genuine acknowledgments of others make a significant difference in their success and in yours. When your individual employees' performance increases, so does the performance of the overall team and, in time, the organization. You'll also benefit from the positive effects. But before you get there, you must remember to stay in the moment and pay attention to the person or people you are trying to inspire. Focus on what they specifically did or said and the specific talents they used well. See what happens when you start noticing the positive actions and talents of others and report to them your observations. The impact will be profound. *Do not underestimate your positive influence on another person.*

After years of coaching, I continue to be surprised by the impact genuine, specific acknowledgments have on others, whether it is my wife, children, friends, or clients. Even the toughest birds respond favorably. The biggest reason, I think, is that my acknowledgments are always genuine. All I do is observe and report those observations. This helps people repeat their outstanding performance and more often use the talents I have cited. This produces greater levels of genuine self-confidence, courage, and grit. You will also find that through acknowledgment, your followers will appreciate you more and be apt to trust and follow you in a way that creates a greater fulfillment, better performance, and high levels of satisfaction—both theirs and your own. When people believe you understand how their talents can be used, they will also return to you time and again to be inspired and work toward the correct solutions and action plans.

> "People may take a job for more money, but they often leave it for more recognition."
> —Bob Nelson, author and motivational speaker

Each person I coach is a successful leader. All are respected for the position they hold and most for who they are as people. When they say something, it has weight, it has gravitas, and it is important to the one who is listening to them. *Whether as a boss, a peer, another employee, a parent, a spouse, or a friend, what you say will be placed quite firmly in the mind of the listener and become a part of their active memory for a long time.* This is especially true when what you say is seen as perceptive and expresses something the person can actively use. A genuine acknowledgment expresses thoughts that can be clearly used.

Each genuine, specific, and thoughtful acknowledgment is like giving the person a medal. Sometimes it is perceived as a gold medal. Those medals are stored in their mind and visualized as a source of confidence and inspiration as they face new and difficult challenges.

> **"Authentic leaders are intentional and strategic with theirrecognition practices. They use recognition to reward, coach, and motivate their people. They know that true recognition goes deeper than the basic 'nice job' and that it requires thoughtfulness and meaning."**
> **—Steve Keating**

There are few people who do not appreciate hearing "nice job" or a variation of those words. And yet to most they can feel like the skeleton of recognition. There is no meat on those bones. It is relatively easy to recognize and acknowledge when the work was done well by saying "nice job." The genuine acknowledgment, in contrast, gives a person something to chew on, to take home, and to use again and again. The key, and source of its power, is that you noticed them and that you took the time to report to them what you observed. Once you start regularly giving genuine acknowledgments, you will be grateful you have inspired someone and they will be grateful for you and inspired to repeat what they did or said.

Before we leave this chapter, keep something in mind as you prepare to give your leaders and employees meaningful acknowledgments: Two things that make them meaningful are the level of detail noted and how the recipient will interpret your comments. For example, "That was a great presentation" is not as powerful as "Great presentation! I like your attention to details. The PowerPoint slides contained dynamic graphics and the incorporation of our brand colors throughout gave it a harmonious theme. I was especially impressed during the Q&A portion; your preparation was evident in your ability to articulately answer the audience's complex questions." With this level of detail, likely what they will hear is: "You are intelligent, engaging, detailed-oriented, meticulous, and a treasure trove of valuable insights. You are the perfect brand ambassador. You fascinate me."

Multiple research studies, including those done by the National Business Research Institute (NBRI), Harvard Medical School, and the Wharton School have shown that a high percentage of employees are much more productive when their talents, behaviors, and accomplishments are specifically acknowledged.

6

Wise and Thoughtful Delegation

No man will make a great leader who wants to do it all himself or to get all the credit for doing it.
—Andrew Carnegie

My client Peter was failing to do the job he was expected to do. He was working too many hours, did not have the time to do the things that were most important for a leader at his level, and was regularly missing deadlines. He was battling fatigue and depression. His role was at the corporate office level. His subordinates were in the field and had a dual reporting relationship to him.

Peter, as a core value, respected others and wanted to be nice to them. His subordinates were loaded with work and he believed it would not be fair to give them more.

He therefore ended up doing the work that had been designed for them. As I coached Peter and asked him questions, he was able to rethink his definition of what "being fair" really is, what his job was supposed to be, what his responsibilities were in using the talents he had, and what it meant to respect his subordinates enough to give them assignments that would stretch them and help them grow in their careers.

After several months of discussion about these issues, a new light appeared in Peter's brain and illuminated what he should be doing for the benefit of everyone, including himself. Although Peter did discover a new way of thinking that turned out to be a great change for him, it was difficult because his previous thinking was strongly ingrained. (We have all experienced that situation.) A new way of thinking required that he reassess how he could maintain and live out his strongly held values—especially to respect and honor others—in a new way. When any of us are trying to change a behavior or way of thinking that has been ingrained in us for many years, it is important to realize that type of change is not just like turning off a light switch. It is going to be challenging and require discipline. It is a personal and internal battle between "What I have been doing or thinking isn't so bad" and "I really want and need to make this change because it is in my best interest (and probably the best interest of a whole lot of other people as well) regardless of how hard it is."

Peter also demonstrated that worrying about what is fair can be a path leading to a lower level of performance and to failure. Considering what is best for each person and the organization is the key consideration. Through delegating when appropriate—not just giving unwanted tasks to others—he discovered that everyone involved became more successful. He was now able to do the things that created the highest value for the organization. His depression and sense of failure was replaced with a genuine sense of satisfaction and optimism. Having made the changes he did, two years later his company won a coveted national award in the area in which he held the principal responsibility.

Before looking more closely at what occurred in the exchange with Peter, let's explore a contrast. The idea of being nice and/or fair brings me to offer a challenge to think about those ideals in a new way. Most of us want to be known as a "fair" person or leader in this world in which we all confront many things that do not seem "fair." What do you suppose the result would be if you became a leader who focuses on what is best for each person and the organization rather than what is fair? Both require a discernment or judgment about what is fair versus what is best for any person. A leader is *expected to exercise wise judgments*, to be discerning. Being fair conjures up a sense of righteousness, of being a good person. In a clarifying shade of contrast, what does it mean to act in the best interests of the other person? In the context of the story about Peter, it means going beyond what seems like the nice, considerate thing to do (i.e., Peter not giving his subordinates more work) to understanding that it actually is in their best interest to give them additional work and therefore that is the nicest thing he can do.

Maybe being nice or fair as a leader, the way we normally think about the meaning of those words, gives the leader a sense of short-term gratification. Determining and doing what is in the best interest of the person has longer-term ramifications for that person and for the company—it is more oriented to the other person and less to oneself. Although there will be more said about this later, please consider the ramifications for you in thinking about what is best for the other person (longer term) rather than what seems like the nice thing to do or to say when engaged in a difficult conversation.

> "It is wonderful when people believe in their leader; but it is more wonderful when the leader believes in the people."
> —John C. Maxwell

In Peter's story, he demonstrated in a new and convincing way that he believed in his subordinates. One of the ways they responded to this was by expanding their ability to do more and perform at a higher level. The story of Peter demonstrates that when you delegate wisely there are many benefits.

The Benefits of Wisely Delegating

More is accomplished when you delegate wisely. As a leader, the more you put everyone in the sweet spots of their talents, including you, the greater the likelihood of achieving short- and long-term exceptional performance. Delegating wisely both develops and uses those talents.

Goals are more likely to be met as well. In a high-performing company, all leaders have specific goals, both quantitative and qualitative. When we thoughtfully delegate, we think mostly about accomplishing a quantitative goal. It is also wise to keep in mind many opportunities to achieve qualitative goals in the process of "making the numbers." It's easy to overlook the skills that were needed to accomplish the goal. In recognizing those skills you inspire their continual use. As people's talents are used and their capabilities are stretched, more gets done and everyone is more likely to be doing what they are paid to do. Of course there are often more risks associated with delegating something important than in doing it yourself. One of the lynchpins of long-term success in business is taking thoughtful risks. Ralph Waldo Emerson was a prime example of equating risks with experiments. He said, "Don't be too timid and squeamish about your actions. All life is an experiment. The more experiments you make the better." Mark Zuckerburg said, "The only strategy that is guaranteed to fail is not taking risks." There are risks in delegating something you can do exceptionally well; yet, when the person clearly understands and has articulated what is to be accomplished, the gains are substantial.

You show your respect and the respect for you as a leader grows. When you delegate to a subordinate, it is implied that you trust them to do the work successfully. You respect them enough to ask them to accomplish the goal. Delegation is a clear and definite demonstration of your respect for that person. And, occasionally, it is wise to be clear about that. One of many ways to do that is to say something like: "I am asking you to do this because I trust you and know it will let you use your naturally strategic mind and your ability to understand and communicate the big picture." In doing this, you will set them up to do better than even *they* thought they could.

The opposite can certainly appear to be true. When you do not appropriately delegate, your subordinate may conjure up the idea that you do not trust him or you do not respect him. And if you actually do not trust or respect him, it is time to replace him *or to start trusting and respecting him*. It is true that as we trust and respect others, they are more likely to trust and respect us.

You give others greater opportunities to learn and excel in their careers. The old adage "You don't know until you try" applies to both a leader and his or her subordinate. You as a leader may be highly confident in a subordinate's ability to accomplish a goal or you may have some doubts. But you will never know until you give that person the opportunity to succeed or fail. That also applies to the one to whom you are delegating. They may be highly confident in their ability or may have some doubts. When you give them trust and respect, they are naturally more motivated to shed their doubts and perform at their highest level.

Barriers to Delegation

Some of the barriers to appropriate and wise delegation include: *wanting to be "nice" (as discussed related to Peter).*

➤ *Thinking you can do the job better than anyone else.* There most likely have been many times when you have thought this. This thinking is natural. If, however, you do develop others' best thinking about the optimal plan, you will have provided your thinking and guidance through the questions you asked. You will have led the subordinate to become far more capable of doing the job exceptionally well. When thinking about delegating, the bigger and wiser question to ask yourself usually is: "Who is the person who should be doing this?" And then, if needed: "What are the trade-offs of asking the best person to do this based on ability versus the best person based on developing and growing them and allowing you to do the things that create the highest value for the company?"

➤ *Not wanting to take the time to explain what you think needs to be done.* It is easy to think that your subordinate should clearly understand what she should do and how she should do it, in many cases without much explanation on your part. "They are smart and should get it." How many times have you explained something and the listener, even the really smart ones, did not "get" what you thought you were communicating? What is the best remedy for that? Is it to take more time to explain and clarify your thoughts? Is it to explain the "why" to them? Or is something else even more effective?

This gets to the heart of some of the earlier stories in this book. When we place the burden on ourselves for being eloquent and crystal clear, failure is much more likely than if we place the burden on ourselves to ask questions that bring out the other person's best thinking about what and how something should be accomplished, and what makes it important to do it and to do it well (the "why"). When they articulate and create it, they own it; they have a much better opportunity to truly understand it and most importantly their confidence in their ability to do a great job soars. *And it all happened because of the thought-provoking questions you asked them.*

A response to this might be, "I don't have the time to ask all the questions. You do not understand how busy I am, how much I have on my plate already!" Yet, if your subordinate truly understands what needs to done, why it needs to done, and how it needs to done and *has articulated that to you*, how much time and frustration on your part would you reckon will be saved?

➤ *Not trusting the person to do the work to be accomplished successfully.* The benefits of trusting someone was discussed earlier, but to put emphasis on this point: There are times when it makes sense to be explicit about your trust in the other person by saying something like: "I have great confidence in your ability to achieve this." And in some cases when giving a boost to their confidence is good, ask the question: "What gives you the most confidence that you can get this done?" And if they miss an important talent they have, say to them and ask them: "That is all true and in what ways do you see your analytical (or your ability to relate to others, etc.) talent being important?"

➤ *Lack of clarity about the goal and what needs to be done to accomplish it.* This relates to the discussion about not wanting to take the time to fully communicate. Lack of clarity about the why, what, and how causes the most failed attempts at delegating. What I said is not what you heard me say and what I say, more often than not, I understand. Therefore, require the one who is going to be responsible for accomplishing the goal verbalize the what, why, and how. Be direct, and when you think there may be some doubt in a person's mind about the "why," ask them: "What makes this so important to (a group, groups of people, the company, etc.)?"

Elizabeth Grace Saunders offers three steps for overcoming the barriers to delegation in her *Forbes* piece of the same name. She details the need to idenfity where to focus and where you, as the leader, can contribute the most value.

To help you let go of projects other people can do, you need to understand what exactly should fill the majority of your time. Where can your contribution make the biggest impact? For most business owners, these activities include strategic thinking about new business opportunities, building relationships, sales, and specific elements of operations.[1]

Understand why you are fearful of delegation. Are you afraid that the work won't get done? Will it not be done to satisfaction? What are the risks to delegating projects or tasks to others? Address the risks. Through disciplined self-exploration, Saunders suggests that you "Figure out how you can minimize the risk when someone else does the work. This will allow you to put the appropriate checks and balances and safeguards into place."

To summarize, keep in mind these factors as you think about delegating significant things that need to be accomplished:

➤ Through your questions, allow the person to own the task and to articulate its importance.

➤ When you delegate, you show you respect and trust the other person.

➤ You will give the other person the opportunity to use their talents and, in some cases, stretch their abilities.

➤ You as a leader will be giving your subordinates a new opportunity to excel.

➤ You have more time to do the things that best fit your talents and the responsibilities of your role.

7

Consistent Accountability

You can't build a reputation on what you're going to do.
—Henry Ford

A client named Dennis told me, "I know I should hold people more accountable, but in my heart, I want to give them a break." Dennis's story was similar to Peter's from Chapter 6. And both of their stories are similar to those I have heard from many other clients. Developing and sustaining a culture of consistent accountability requires much of you as a leader, and its development is made easier by actively using the skills discussed in this book. Let's start, however, with what it might look like in your organization.

As leaders, we get what we model. An organization with a culture of consistent accountability is populated with people who accomplish the goals they agree to accomplish within the time they say they will get it done. That is clearly easier to state than to do. Please note the emphasis is on what is *accomplished* in contrast to effort or tasks. Everyone's commitment is to successfully accomplish what they said they would accomplish. As leaders, we get what we model. As the leader, followers in the organization hear what you say through their own filters and pay close attention to what you do. As you model personal accountability and are *consistent* in requiring accountability from everyone equally, your actions have a ripple effect throughout the entire organization. People follow what you do more than what they hear you say. One of the keys here is that you are consistent.

When we fail to hold some subordinates accountable, we signal to them that our expectations of them personally are less than others and it stifles their highest performance. Those who are held accountable feel that it is wrong to give anyone a pass, especially when they never receive one.

Action Step

For just one month hold all your direct reports accountable for what they commit to do without any variance based on whether they are a high or low performer. See if you signal higher expectations and the performance of both groups increases. As consistent accountability becomes the standard by which you lead, everyone involved will meet these higher expectations. As their performance increases, you'll see an obvious change in attitudes, modes of working, and morale. In the process, you're doing more than just "helping" your team—you're fostering an overall culture of accountability.

Key Elements to a Consistent Accountability Culture

Commitment and Trust

John Maxwell said: "When you make a commitment you create hope. When you keep a commitment, you create trust." Every time I coach an executive team the goal is to help them become an even higher performing team. It is about creating a higher level of measurable performance and results. A great team becomes high-performing when there is full trust—and trust is built on everyone doing what they say they will do in the time they said they will do it. In four words: Everyone Keeps Their Commitments. As a leader, what else can you commit to in order to model a culture in which everyone meets their commitments?

Clear Expectations

We all have experienced times when we thought it was clear that we said X was going to be done in Y time period and the person most responsible (PMR) was equally clear that she was going to do Z or X+2 in the W time period. In the chapters on developing others' best thinking and delegation there was a discussion about the power of the PMR for accomplishing the goal, articulating that goal (saying it out loud) to you as the leader, and then that person creating their own deadline, with which you fully concur. Expectations have the highest chance to be met when the person clearly says what they will do and when it will be completed. Additionally, if there seems to be any question in that person's mind related to the importance or the significance of achieving the goal, ask them something like: "When you think about it, what makes achieving this goal in the time period you've committed to so important?" This helps them to articulate and form a stronger commitment to getting it done in the time period they have established. Again, they are telling themselves in their own words rather than you telling them.

Ability

It is clear that when you hold someone accountable, you must have the belief that they have the ability to get it done—to reach the goal. Talent, experience, drive, motivation, creativity, willingness to stretch, and self-awareness all drive the ability to produce the desired result. Self-awareness and knowing the talents of your team members come into play when and if you should decide what you should personally do and what should be delegated.

Measure Results and Set Timelines

When you have discretion on timelines you may be surprised at the results when you ask the PMR for accomplishing the goal what he or she thinks the timeline for completion should be rather than setting it yourself. The principle here is the same as it is with allowing the person to own the solution. When the PMR sets the timeline, he or she owns it. It becomes theirs. Often someone else or factors outside of your control determine deadlines. When that is the case, it is also wise to ask the PMR something like: "Given this has to be completed by July 25th, what will be the best ways to measure the progress and what should be the timelines?" If the PMR's responses are not on target or what they need to be, the next question states the issue and still gives the PMR the opportunity to verbalize what the timeline needs to be. For example, "If the initial marketing plan is completed by July 15, how will the Division and Corporate office reviewers react to having a very short time to review it and get it back to you?" Through your questions you cause them to think through and verbalize the ramifications they missed.

One of the key points here is that you, as the leader, are fostering the other person's best thinking through the questions you ask. When something is said related to the solution or timeline that does not make sense to you, ask another question that brings light to the issue you see. That way the PMR still articulates "the answer" and owns it. You will find that once you start practicing this approach, the process takes little time. What little time it does take is far outweighed by the benefits of a greater understanding of the solution, the action plan, and the importance of achieving the goal (the why) and the timelines.

Understand the Personal Consequences of Failure

It is essential that we all understand why it is in our personal best interest to do just about anything, and do it well. Oftentimes the understanding of why something we do or say is in our best interest is subconscious. When we can explain to ourselves or another person, we are much better armed with the grit and tenacity to accomplish any goal. In a culture of consistent accountability, people can explain with conviction why it is best for them personally to work in an organization in which they and everyone else are held consistently accountable for accomplishing what they created as their own goal. With the foundation of understanding the personal benefits of being accountable, it is always wise to be aware when you should ask the seemingly pointed question "For you personally, what should be the consequences of not getting this done successfully in the time you have laid out?" As you consider asking this question, why do you think it is more effective that your subordinate tell you what the consequence should be rather than you telling him or her what that consequence is? If you ask the question about consequences, as with all other situations in which you ask the other person to articulate their thoughts, ask follow-up questions that start with "what" when they missed a key point.

Establish a Culture of Accountability

Even in an organization that emphasizes a culture of accountability, there will still be some uncontrollable events—though they are rare exceptions. Common sense, thoughtfulness, and grace will never be discounted. However, based on my observations of hundreds of companies, they are usually identified as either having a culture of *exceptions and circumstances* or a culture of *accountability*. There is little middle ground.

How the leaders and employees describe and think about the culture of your organization is key because it promulgates the culture that is considered to be acceptable. What is the norm for your company? Think of the reality of your company's culture as a fulcrum. Is it clearly weighted with a culture of accountability or a culture of exceptions and reasons as to why things don't get done? Or is it like a teeter-totter? One day it seems like it is weighted toward accountability and the next day it is not.

Just as the CEO can model consistent accountability for the entire organization, the leader of a subset of the organization can also model and establish that type of culture within his or her own organization. If you are a leader within just one part of the company, boldly create your own culture of accountability. To accomplish that, the people in your organization will need to articulate why that will be beneficial to them personally.

Clear accountabilities are one of the fundamentals of a team acting as a team and striving to accomplish the same goal. Teams that demonstrate a high level of consistent accountability have a higher level of trust among each other.

As an extension, in a company with a culture of consistent accountability there will rarely be a meeting that does not end with everyone clearly understanding their accountabilities. How many meetings have you attended and thought at the end, "That was a nice discussion, but what did we accomplish?" The answer is "nothing." Meetings that are worth everyone's time will move the ball forward. Everyone will know at the close of the meeting what he or she is committed to do and the deadline to accomplish the job at hand.

> **No meeting should end without specific,**
> **clear accountabilities and timelines.**

Everyone involved wants to have the sense that they are moving in a positive and productive way to reach the goals discussed—it seems inherent in all of us and it gives us energy to know what we need to do and what others are doing. *Teams that demonstrate a high level of consistent accountability correspondingly develop a high level of trust in each other.* They can trust that their teammate will do what they said they were going to do and a culture of accountability will persist.

Joseph Folkman, in his article in the November 14, 2014 edition of *Forbes* titled "The 8 Great Accountability Skills for Business Success" provides some additional thoughts. He says the eight characteristics to create and sustain a culture of accountability are:

1. Drive for Results. His point here is that priorities and expectations must be clear and the person most responsible should have appropriate control. This certainly is in sync with the idea of

having that person articulate what they will do and why what they are doing is important.

2. Honesty and Integrity. It is important that people honestly report their challenges and progress. I would add that honesty and integrity are a function of the character of both the boss and subordinate. What culture have you created related to honesty? What are the consequences in your organization if someone is honest about their failures?

3. Trust. We have discussed trust as it relates to trusting others to do what they say they will do. What role does being a person of good character and being trustworthy, have in your organization? What can you do to further create a culture in which people do genuinely trust each other?

4. Clear Vision and Direction. Folkman cites an old Chinese proverb: "The hunter that chases two rabbits catches neither one." Simply put, like multitasking when you're listening, focusing on one rabbit at a time yields results. Focusing on that one rabbit does not mean that multiple things won't be accomplished on the way to catching it or shooting it.

5.   Problem-Solving and Technical Expertise. People obviously need to have the skills and ability to accomplish the goal. As they articulate their solution and plans, it will become clearer if that is the case.

6.   Communication. Folkman says "When a leader can effectively communicate, others can understand what they are accountable for. This requires being able to tell, ask, and listen to others." As discussed earlier, the most effective communication comes from asking, listening, asking, listening, asking, listening, and doing some telling (directing) along the way.

7.   Ability to Change. This book is about change. Change that will have great benefits for you and all those with whom you interact. Folkman found that "People who are really good at creating change in an organization had employees operating at a higher level." As advocated in this book, the probability of a person changing their thinking or behavior is much greater when they say out loud what is in their best interest to change and why that is important to them rather than the leader telling them.

8. Collaboration and Resolving Conflicts. Folkman asks the question, "Are you cooperating or competing with others in your group?" I have very successful clients who do both. In a culture of consistent accountability both can thrive. Much depends on what is driving each employee. If you as a leader have inspired them to believe that as the organization thrives and each person is successful they will flourish, they will want their piece of the company to be successful and will compete and, at the same time will know cooperation and collaboration is essential for the company to be successful.

HCA is one the United States's most skillfully managed companies. They operate 179 hospitals and 120 free-standing surgery centers, have 240,000 employees, and had $44 billion in revenue in 2017. They were again named one of Ethisphere Institute's World Most Ethical Companies in 2017. They are recognized as having a culture of consistent accountability.

Some of the major factors that promote a culture of consistent accountability are:

> Emphasis on making sure all goals are clearly understood.

> ➤ Providing timely data related to the progress in achieving goals. (HCA is a data rich company.)

> ➤ Transparency around achievement of meeting key goals.

> ➤ Person-to-person reviews of the progress in meeting the goals.

> ➤ Clear and practical action plans coming out of these meetings.

> ➤ Hiring and promoting with a major emphasis on being accountable.

> ➤ Little tolerance for chronic lack of accountability.

If you wish to inspire your organization to have, or become more clearly, a culture of accountability, in what ways could these key elements be helpful to you?

Barriers to Creating a Culture of Accountability

Over the years, I have coached several leaders who get into the habit of finishing what others committed to do. They take the "easier" path. Rather than confronting the person who did not do what they said they would do and spend the energy to hold him or her accountable, they just do it themselves. They then end up wondering why they are working so many hours and do not have the time to use their own talent and to lead (just like Bob, who we met earlier in the book). When they start holding others consistently accountable for what they have committed to accomplish, however, the effect on them and their subordinates is profoundly positive.

> "Obstacles are those frightful things you see when you take your eyes off your goal."
> —Henry Ford

Still, many of the leaders I have coached have some reluctance to hold others consistently responsible. The three most prevalent reasons are that they:

1. Want to be a nice and considerate person. The leader who wants to be nice and considerate should look at what that means from a different perspective. We covered the distinction in the last chapter: It actually is "nice" to hold others to a high standard of performance, even when it may not feel this is the case in the moment.

2. Can perform the task or action faster and better. A leader's ability to do a task better and faster than a subordinate may well be true. Yet that

creates major barriers to do what you are really paid to do—to create the highest value for the organization. Many of the leaders who I have coached have been surprised when they overcame this obstacle. Their subordinate accomplished the goal, but might have gotten there with a different style or process.

3. Lack confidence that another person can accomplish the goal as well as it should be done. This, like the preceding reason, is mostly a matter of giving up perceived control and taking risks. When you as a leader are wondering about a subordinate's ability to reach a goal, spend a little bit more time leading the person through the questions you ask so that they tell you the highlights of what they need to do to be successful. Remind them of the talents they have and ask them in what ways they can most effectively use those talents to accomplish the goal. This again sounds like it will consume more time than you want to give it or that you have. If you have those thoughts, please think through all the benefits that will accrue if you take the extra time. It is a short-term bump for a long-term benefit.

Inspire Consistent Accountability and the Results

As you hold others accountable you show you trust and respect them, their decisions, and their actions. This also signals that you have high expectations for them and you believe in their ability to accomplish the goal. They may end up thinking, "Wow, boss, if you think I can do this, then I should think I can too." You are giving them more opportunities to grow in their thinking and in their career, while building their confidence and helping the company succeed.

As you actively think of the positive effects on followers of holding them consistently accountable—respecting, honoring, valuing, enhancing their career, and building their confidence—it becomes not only the smart thing to do, but also the right thing to do. When holding others accountable, you are inspiring them in a positive way.

When *you* tell a person what they will be accountable for and the required timelines, it can feel satisfying and efficient to you. You tell them exactly what to do and now it is off your plate. However, when you lead followers to create their own sense of urgency—as discussed earlier—

and to accept accountability for their actions, they have the pride of ownership of the plan and the additional responsibility that comes from creating their own responsibilities and timeline. You have not imposed it on them; they have imposed it upon themselves.

To accomplish this simply ask the other person, "What timeline makes the most sense for you and for the business?" If the timeline they give is too long, ask something like, "If the timeline is extended to that date, what are the implications for the people most affected, or for the employees, or for the customer, or to accomplish the larger goal (or whatever is at the heart of your concern)?" The idea is that you target the issue you see in the extended timeline by asking an open-ended question.

When you hold others accountable the affect goes beyond you. When you as a leader consistently hold your direct reports accountable, they will more naturally hold their subordinates consistently accountable too. You model the behavior, and they will in turn model it as well. Everyone in the organization will begin to learn that the new reality is that they must do what they committed to do in the agreed-upon time. In so doing, everyone will believe they are respected and valued by their bosses and a culture of accountability will take root.

When you hold others consistently accountable:

➤ You clearly show your respect for and your trust in the person.

➤ You as the leader gain a greater level of respect.

➤ The frequency of goals being accomplished well and on time dramatically increases.

➤ You have more time to think, to lead, and do the things that provide your company with the greatest benefit.

➤ Your employees' satisfaction increases along with their confidence because they feel a greater sense of personal value from accomplishing what they said they'd do in the time period they said they'd do it.

➤ Your personal success and the company's success is elevated.

Conclusion

Challenges and Rewards

It has been a privilege to help a large number of senior executives think through the implications and benefits of consistently using the basic skills discussed in this book. Without exception, it has been a great challenge for each person to think anew about more successful ways to lead and to form new habits. Everyone is tested as they muster the required focus and discipline to reap the extraordinary rewards that come with actively focusing on using each of the skills. Every client I have worked with says it is hard to become a better listener, to inspire others through genuine acknowledgments, to ask many more thoughtful and powerful questions, to bring out the best thinking of others rather than sharing their best thinking and then asking what the other person thinks, to hold themselves and others consistently accountable, and to more actively delegate with wisdom.

> **Put the interests of others in a paramount position.**
> **As you thoughtfully do that, your personal success thrives,**
> **maybe in ways that you could not imagine.**

Every one of my clients who has focused on using these skills has reported higher levels of performance for them, for their team, and for their entire organization. They feel an incredible satisfaction that comes from inspiring others to fully use their talents and achieve exceptional results—and find that the more they exercise these skills the more time they have to think and soar as a leader.

The thread going through everything in this book is: As you respect others and *put the interests of others in a paramount position, your personal success thrives, maybe in ways that you could not imagine.* As this is being written, millions of people around the world are celebrating the life of Billy Graham and, more importantly, how he lived his life as a follower of Jesus. He has been noted for his honesty and integrity, for fully living what he preached, his extraordinary speaking ability, his ability to inspire millions of people to believe in Christ, his complete fidelity to his beliefs, and deep and genuine humility. Another attribute that had a strong impact on me was that he lived his life never worrying about or focusing on his own success. Billy Graham focused all his attention on the success of others. He respected and honored all people. Although not focusing on his personal success, it is clear that he was the most successful person in his field throughout the past two centuries. What are the possibilities for you if you also shine the spotlight on others, putting their interests before yours?

As my clients work to better understand their values and what they want to be as a leader, many find that respecting their team members, colleagues, and coworkers take on a greater focus. If it is important to you to respect all other people, using these skills becomes easier. Each one has an inherent component of respect for the other person. Although this is most clear in listening, executing all of the skills is a powerful demonstration of your respect for the other person. And the flip side of that seems to be true: When you do not actively use these skills, you disrespect others. If respecting another person is important to you, ask yourself after each encounter with another person: "In what ways did I demonstrate that I respected that person?"

As a way to live out your values, try this exercise. For one month, measure the level of respect you gave to each person you encountered. Be clear in your own mind that consistently having high expectations for their level of performance signals your respect for them and your strong will to help them thrive. Then, see if you can actively demonstrate that you care about the success of each person. I have seen amazing changes in performance when a leader leads with the primary goal of making everyone around him or her successful. In the process, the leader gains a new and more significant sense of gratitude and personal fulfillment. I am not advocating that the leader be "nice" or "soft." In fact, when the interest of others is paramount in your mind and actions, you may be known as a tough boss. The people who we respect, admire, appreciate, and want to follow are those who have high expectations for us and help us meet their high expectations. With a clear sense of respect and personal interest in us, they demand the best from us. And, it may be on occasion that helping a person get another job inside or outside of the company will be the best gift on another person's path to success.

I was given that gift early in my career. My talents did not match the job I had as the controller and chief of finance. I was in the wrong job. The president, who was also the owner of the company, and I jointly reached the conclusion that I should seek another company and another job. Although it was amicable, I was fired! And I was given a new opportunity to use my talents and develop them into real strengths. To use my talents more fully, I chose a business in which I had no experience and started my own company. Because my old boss fired me, I was given the chance to serve others and gain success in a business that was well suited to the talents I was given: executive search. And then, over a longer period of time, I continued to gravitate toward using my talents to coach others, which led me to coaching leaders full time. It turned out the president/owner of the company, whether intentionally or not, did have my interests as well as his company's in mind.

Although I have stressed that becoming an exceptional leader requires difficult change (even for leaders with well-earned reputations for being no-nonsense, blunt, get-it-done-now, I am and will be the smartest "guy" in the room), change can occur. A redirection of thinking is required. The first is to rethink the smartest way for you to lead. You can be successful for some period of time by being the obvious smart one and weigh in whenever "needed" to demonstrate your intelligence. Typically, this approach limits others' abilities and your own success as the leader. The other approach is to start bringing out more decisively the intelligence and best thinking of others. Rethink which will bring the greatest level of results for you and for your followers—you'll find that consistently expecting and requiring your subordinates' best thinking will lead to breakthroughs in their own performance.

It is both intuitive and has been demonstrated by each of my clients that through great questions, one is able to bring out others' best thinking. As that is done consistently, their performance and your success substantially increases. They know you are smart. You no longer have to prove it and they will start thinking you are even smarter because you bring out the best in them. Asking powerful questions challenges and inspires your followers. Understand that for just about every leader, asking more questions that begin with "what," practicing focused listening, and giving genuine acknowledgment are difficult changes to make. The reward comes with sustained focus and tenacity.

As you start to focus on using the skills discussed in this book, you will be grateful you did!

Practical Suggestions

Keep Track

Figure out the best way for you to measure your success. For many of my clients it has been helpful to keep a log for a few weeks to maintain focus. Before a meeting, you may want to do something as simple as putting at the top of a notebook page, pad, or agenda, something like:

➤ L (Listened rather than talked).

➤ Q (Asked great questions).

➤ GA (Provided genuine and specific acknowledgments).

➤ ACC (Ended the meeting with clear accountabilities related to each action item).

Then add tick marks each time you followed through on each action. Write each of the skills on a note card and keep them where you can easily see them to keep you focused. At the end of each day, grade yourself. Ask one or more people with whom you are comfortable sharing to pay close attention to your actions and provide you with periodic feedback.

Accountability Partner

Due to the difficulty of focusing on making the changes needed to hone these skills, many of my clients have asked someone, or a few people, to be their observer: a trusted person, usually peers or subordinates, to more closely take note of their use of all the skills and periodically report what they have noticed. It is not a formal reporting, but it is a good way to stay focused and gain feedback. It also helps those giving you feedback to more closely notice their own use of the skills. Additionally, it demonstrates your level of genuine self-confidence to ask for this kind of feedback and gives your observers an even clearer sense that you trust and respect them.

Intentional Peer Practice

As a part of the program I offer to leadership teams, I demonstrate the use of the skills for fifteen minutes with the leader of the team as he or she discusses a real challenge or opportunity they face. Each of the participants pairs with another participant and for fifteen minutes practices the use of all of the skills as they help the person with whom they are paired reach a solution and action plan for the challenge or opportunity they have presented. (All of the participants have noted what progress can be made in just fifteen minutes.) These exercises are done in the first session and then in the three following sessions. Beyond practicing the use of the skills and the recognition for their value, they come to better understand that a person can help you solve a challenge without being an expert in the subject area. They are then encouraged to continue practicing the skills with a team member as they talk with that person about a business challenge they have. As an unexpected benefit, the level of trust and respect increases between the two team members during this exercise.

Feel grateful that what you are doing will be positive for *everyone* with whom you interact because you put others paramount to yourself. This simple yet challenging principle has the power to not only transform you and your team, but all with whom you come into contact.

As I coached more and more individuals and teams to inspire the use of these skills and saw the results, my passion grew to communicate them to others. The results were personal for each person, not only in the impact it had on their leadership of others, but in their life with their family and with their friends. It is in that spirit that I was motivated to write this book. On this journey, I discovered writing is not a natural talent for me. So, the four-year journey to complete it was a bit of a struggle. Adopting an approach of pretending I was speaking rather than writing was helpful.

My bottom-line hope is that you will use the thoughts presented in this book to be more of the person and the leader you were meant to be. None of it is particularly easy. If you work hard on using these skills as I have as a coach, you will be grateful you did and amazed with the truly incredible results.

Appendix

Sample Questions

Make these questions your own and keep in mind that, after you ask any of these questions, follow-up questions may be needed to continue to bring out the very best thinking of the best who you are leading. Although some of the questions may appear to be somewhat awkward or too penetrating, you will be pleased with the results they will create.

Inspire and Create High Expectations

➤ What are the highest expectations you have for yourself related to the issue/challenge at hand?

- ➤ What do you think my expectations of you should be related to the success you achieve with each goal or for your performance?

- ➤ If you achieve that success, what impact will it have on you?

- ➤ In what ways can you more fully apply/use your strengths in achieving the outcome you want?

- ➤ What are you doing or could you do to make you feel great about the work you are doing?

- ➤ What else do you need to do to achieve tremendous success?

- ➤ What is your best thinking related to this?

- ➤ In what new ways could your experience be used?

- ➤ In what ways could you really make a positive difference?

- ➤ What leadership skills will be most important in tackling this opportunity?

- ➤ If you "go for the gold," what will happen?

- ➤ If the goal is fully met, what will give you the most gratitude about the achievement?

➤ What makes this matter for you?

➤ What will be the impact when you do a great job with this? Or when you reach your goal?

➤ What is your sense of why this is important?

Get Unstuck When Dealing With a Tough Challenge

➤ What is at the heart of this situation?

➤ What is the *real* issue here?

➤ What is the one thing you know about this challenge/opportunity?

➤ What is it about that one thing that can help you formulate a solution?

➤ If you took a small step, what would it be?

➤ What does your gut tell you about this?

➤ What should be your real goal here?

➤ What are your best insights so far?

➤ If you were to just think creatively, not worrying about practicality, what would you be thinking?

Develop Another Person's Best Thinking

➤ What is the most important objective?

➤ What else do you know about this?

➤ If you were to think out of the box, what would you be thinking?

➤ What is your biggest concern?

➤ What is the one concrete and positive thing you can do to lessen that concern?

➤ What do you think is really going on here?

➤ If you put yourself in the other person's shoes, what would you be thinking?

➤ When you peel away the layers, what really matters here (in this particular situation or issue)?

➤ When you peel away the layers, what is at the heart of this?

➤ If you focus on what you know, in contrast to what you think you know, what pieces are most relevant?

➤ What is the sub-plot?

➤ What is the key player's motivation in this?

➤ What key factors are currently driving this?

Help Others Become Successful Leaders

➤ What are the crucial measurements of your success?

➤ In what ways would it be good to think more about what those measurements should be for you?

➤ As you reflect on your experiences, assessments you have taken, and feedback you have received, what talents and skills do you have that are most important for you to be an exceptionally high performer in your current job?

➤ What is the allocation of your time between doing, delegating, and inspiring?

➤ What difference would it make in your ability to become an even greater leader if your active listening skills were considerably sharpened?

➤ What difference would it make in your ability to become an even greater leader if you consistently asked great questions?

➤ What difference would it make in your ability to become an even greater leader if you encourage the best thinking of others as a result of your active listening and great questions?

➤ What would be the effect on a subordinate's motivation and confidence if you brought out their best thinking rather than telling them what to do or think?

➤ What difference would it make in your ability to become an even greater leader if you were effective at providing others genuine acknowledgments of what they did or said?

➤ What difference would it make in your ability to become an even greater leader if you held others consistently accountable?

➤ What would the affect be on successfully doing your job if you delegated more thoughtfully and wisely?

Help a Person Motivate and Inspire Someone Who Is Both Difficult and Important to the Business

➤ What is your sense of what he or she thinks success is?

➤ What seems to set him or her off and what practical and wise things could you do to minimize that?

➤ What seems to motivate him or her?

➤ Who, if anyone, relates well to them and what is that person doing that you might emulate?

➤ What do you think is at the heart of his or her difficult/bad/negative behavior or actions?

➤ What is one thing that might make a difference that you control and could do to change his or her thinking and behavior?

➤ As you think about that person, what are their positive traits and talents?

➤ What would be the benefit for you and the other person if you genuinely acknowledged that person when he or she says something or does something that is positive?

➤ In what ways could that change the dynamics of the relationship?

➤ What would be different if you were even more successful in staying focused on the things that jointly benefit you and the other person?

➤ In what ways would your thinking need to change to accomplish that?

Notes

Chapter 1

1. *www.wsj.com/articles/how-active-listening-makes-both-sides-of-a-conversation-feel-better-1421082684*

Chapter 2

1. Letter to Carl Seelig (11 March 1952), Einstein Archives 39-013.

2. *https://hbr.org/2014/08/curiosity-is-as-important-as-intelligence*

3. Grohol, Become a Better Listener, *https://psychcentral.com/lib/author/grohol/*

Chapter 3

1. Thomas Nelson, Developing the Leader Within You, December 2000, page 83.

2. Men, Ideas, and Politics, Harvard Business Review Press, October 25, 2010

3. Jack Welch, Winning, HarperBusiness, April 2005, page 64.

4. *www.criticalthinking.org/pages/the-critical-mind-is-a-questioning-mind/481*

Chapter 5

1. *www.forbes.com/sitesisabellaclivilezwu/2016/07/26/how-you-can-inspire-throughacknowledgement/#1df302ec2b62*

Chapter 6

1. *www.forbes.com/sites/yec/2013/10/31/three-steps-to-overcome-your-fear-of-delegation/#6a16960576f6*

Index